DAFFY

The Autobiography of Phil DeFreitas

DAFFY

The Autobiography of Phil DeFreitas

PHIL DEFREITAS

WITH DEREK CLEMENTS

FOREWORD BY SIR TREVOR McDONALD

APEX PUBLISHING LTD

First published in 2012 by
Apex Publishing Ltd
PO Box 7086, Clacton on Sea, Essex, CO15 5WN

www.apexpublishing.co.uk

Copyright © 2012 by Phil DeFreitas and Derek Clements
The author has asserted their moral rights

British Library Cataloguing-in-Publication Data
A catalogue record for this book
is available from the British Library

ISBN 1-906358-91-5
978-1-906358-91-4

Typeset in 10pt Baskerville Win95BT

Production Manager: Chris Cowlin

Front cover photo supplied by Phil DeFreitas,
back cover photo supplied by Sporting Heroes

Printed and bound by
MPG Books Group in the UK

I dedicate this book to my grandmother, Matilda Henrietta John-Lewis, who was a very special lady in my life. I will never forget her.

CONTENTS

FOREWORD

When I was growing up, cricket was regarded as a West Indian addiction for which there was no known cure. It was the only game in town. When the West Indies team used to tour Australia, I would listen to the match commentary on the radio – the problem was that because of the time difference it meant many late nights. And to make matters worse, I used to listen to the games on a neighbour's radio and wouldn't get home until after midnight – this eventually persuaded my father to go out and buy a radio. I might still be up late listening to the exploits of my heroes, but at least I was under my own roof and he knew precisely where I was.

I had many heroes. I suppose that my first was Frank Worrell, who was both a stylish batsman and a very useful seam bowler, not to mention being West Indies' first black captain – something we all regarded as being very important back home.

As the years passed, I also loved watching the likes of Sir Garfield Sobers, Clive Lloyd and Viv Richards, who were all wonderful cricketers, capable of turning a match with a few spellbinding flashes of the bat.

In more recent years, I did, of course, start to follow English cricket and I always admired Phil DeFreitas. For me, he summed up what a fast bowler should be all about – he had the look, the aggression and the energy and, make no mistake about it, he possessed a wonderful bouncer. He was a very classy bowler and, on his day, he was just about unplayable and had batsmen hopping about all over the place in their crease.

There is little doubt in my mind that if he played for England now he would have won many more caps than he did because he would have been given the time to develop as both a bowler and a batsman. I think he felt that he was always under pressure to succeed and that if he ever failed to take a hatful of wickets then he would be dropped – and that is precisely what happened to him. Now, he would be told to just relax, go out there and play, and he would have delivered. I have no doubts about that.

He is a lovely, gentle and charming man whose smile lights up a room, and he also possesses a great generosity of spirit. When he played cricket, he wanted to win, but off the pitch he was a gentleman, and that is a rare combination in this day and age. It is that warmth and generosity of spirit that really makes him stand out for me, mainly because it is so unusual to come across that in modern sportsmen.

I should also say that, even though he is now in his forties, he still looks like he could bowl as well as ever for his country.

It is a privilege and a pleasure to be asked to write the foreword for Phil's book – his story is a compelling one and I know that you will enjoy reading it. I certainly will."

Sir Trevor McDonald

PREFACE

"I am soft. I had a front when I played cricket, but I have never been hard and I am a very insecure person. I am shy and I am somebody who has been hurt many times in my life."

I first tried to write my life story in 2003 but although I kept coming back to it, I just didn't feel that I was in the right place to do it back then. Apart from anything else, I was still playing and that always seemed to get in the way.

Now I have retired, I am in a good place in my life and it feels like the right time. I want to write it because I have always felt that I have a story that is worth telling. One of the things that has always annoyed me is when somebody has a bit of success and then brings out an autobiography while they are still in their early 20s and haven't lived life at all and don't have a story to tell.

I have played with and against some remarkable cricketers and the game also brought me into contact with some quite incredible people – individuals I would never have met had I not been a professional cricketer.

Through writing this book I have had to face up to one or two uncomfortable truths, and I am sure you will read some things about me in the pages that follow that may well surprise you. I have tried to give an honest and frank account of my life and career, but if you are looking for any sensationalism then you are reading the wrong book.

This is the time to talk about the people who have influenced my life and career, such as Ellis Williams, a PE teacher, who encouraged and supported me at school, and helped me through some very tough times. When I left school I would often go back just to talk to him, about anything at all; then there was Ken Higgs, a great cricketer, a first-class coach and a thoroughly decent man – he was the Leicestershire coach when I first joined and he pushed me and pushed me and was consistently honest to me. Ken was the man who called me 'Half Choc' and called Chris Lewis 'Full Choc' - now that might well seem offensive, racist even, but it wasn't. It was a term of endearment and neither of us was ever offended by it. Geoffrey Boycott called me the same thing and it never offended me coming from him either.

Gatts (former England captain Mike Gatting) and Mickey Stewart were also huge positive influences on my life when I was called into the England Test squad at the age of 20. They looked after me, treated me with respect and handled me wonderfully well on a tour that could have been overwhelming for me. Mickey was a very caring man, as well as being a great coach, and he became like a father figure to me, while Gatts, although captain of England, went out of his way to treat me like a friend. They both made me feel special.

And I couldn't possibly write my life story without mention of David Hughes, who was captain of Lancashire when I joined the county His man-management skills were wonderful and he worked very hard with me to turn me into the cricketer I became. He was the sort of man who, if he sensed that I wasn't happy, would come round to my house to speak to me, to find out what was wrong and whether he could do anything to help. David never got the credit he deserved.

There was one occasion, before a cup match, we were playing against Middlesex and the team talk went along the lines of: "Come on guys, let's go out and beat these southern b******s!" I had been brought up in London and considered myself to be a southerner, so I stood up and said something like: "You can't say that." I look back on it now and realise how silly it all was, but it didn't stop me storming off after the game. David came round to see me and sat me down and explained that it wasn't meant as a slight. It was simply a way of geeing up the boys. It was me being naïve and silly, and I realised that after I spoke with him.

I will tell you what it felt like to be mentally bullied as a teenager, talk in detail about my difficult relationship with my father and try to describe what it was like to be picked by England to tour Australia as a 20-year-old. You will also read about some of the incredible people I have met, from Elton John to Mother Teresa. I even got to shadow box with the one and only Muhammad Ali. And I will take you through my county career, much of which I loved, but parts of which I would not wish upon anybody.

Yes, there have been some personal mistakes, but I have always tried to address those and hold my head up. It may surprise you to learn that I am shy and reserved. It will not surprise you to learn that I could never quite understand why I seemed to be singled out as the scapegoat for England on so many occasions. If I was beginning my career today, I am certain that I would have been treated differently and that I would have been given the opportunity to grow into the team. But it wasn't to be.

Nevertheless, there were some astonishing times, shared with larger-than-life characters such as Ian Botham, Allan Lamb and David Gower who were all as remarkable as you would expect them to have been. Botham's capacity to consume alcohol was just astonishing, but when it came to the business of playing for his country, he was always ready to do his bit. He also had this amazing ability to bowl out leading batsmen with what even he would admit were rank bad deliveries.

If you enjoy reading about these guys as much I did writing about them and about the part they played in my life and career, then I have achieved what I set out to do.

The following pages will take you through more than 40 years of my life. It is far more than a cricketing book. Hopefully, by the time you reach the end you will feel that you know a bit more about what makes me tick and you will realise that I had to do things the hard way. I don't want anybody to feel sorry for me, but I do hope that my story just might inspire one or two youngsters to go out there and prove a point.

I was asked to sum myself up for this book and this is what I said: "I believe that I am a caring, sensitive person. I have always wanted to see the good in people, and still do. People make mistakes as they go through life but as long as they learn from those mistakes that is fine by me – then they can move on. I don't like people being judge. For me, it is important to really sit down and talk to people to get to know them properly.

"I am soft. I had a front when I played cricket, but I have never been hard and I am a very insecure person. I am shy and I am somebody who has been hurt many times in my life."

So there you have it.

I have been hurt many times in my life, and that has made me the man I am today and explains why I am perhaps quite defensive. People don't stop and think about how what they do or say impacts on individuals.

But I have always regarded myself as a fighter. If you are told that you are not good enough, there is no reason why you should accept it. Keep battling, keep plugging away. You will know, deep within yourself, whether or not you are good enough to make it in whatever path you choose to follow.

We all need some breaks along the way, but the key is to work hard and to be able to sit down and the end of each day and know that you have tried your best. Nobody can ask any more of you.

CHAPTER 1
YOU'RE IN SON

My first full season in county cricket was 1986. I was 20 years old, took a lot of wickets and scored a good few runs for Leicestershire and earned the princely sum of £2,000 for the season. The previous year I had been chosen to play in maybe 50% of the first team's matches and still felt very much like an outsider trying to make his way in the game, trying to prove myself to a team full of established professional cricketers.

Remember that this was a side that included David Gower and Peter Willey. They both recognised pretty early on that I was a decent fielder, so although I spent most of the County Championship season as 12th man, I got to take part in a good few of the one-day games, which gave me a taste of what it was all about.

Sitting around with my feet up at the end of the 1985 season wasn't an option. Apart from the fact that I couldn't afford to do nothing, I didn't want to. I knew that I needed to do something to help me develop my game and that the best way to do it was by spending the winter playing in Australia. James Whittaker, one of my teammates, had already been to Australia and I asked him if he could help to fix me up with a club. I discovered that Port Adelaide were looking for an overseas player, so I got on a plane, found my way there and arrived, not knowing a soul.

Port Adelaide gave me a contract and I moved into a flat above a pub, and for the next six months I set about learning my craft.

We trained two or three times a week and played cricket at the weekend – for the rest of my time, I just sat around and twiddled my thumbs, looking forward to my next training session or my next match. Gradually, however, I began to meet people, got to know them socially and was asked round to their houses. Before long, I had a good circle of friends and I was loving the life.

Grade cricket in Australia is no mug's game, and you have to know what you are doing to come out the other side. There were no easy games, and it helped me to grow up. Nobody helped me; I did it all by myself. It would be all too easy for a teenager to go Down Under, have a great time, drink too much beer and learn nothing. Not me though. My purpose in going was to improve all parts of my game, and that is what I did. Cricket was the most important thing in my life, after all.

It meant that when the1986 domestic season began, I was ready for it. In no time at all, I established myself in the first team, and played in every game. I loved every minute of it, taking 90-odd wickets and scoring almost 1,000 runs. I have never found it particularly easy to mix with people, and can identify in many ways with what Marcus Trescothick went through with his depression. In the end, it affected him so badly that he had to quit international cricket at a time when he was the best opening batsman in England and maybe even in the world.

What made the difference for me was that because I quickly got into my stride and played a real part in helping Leicestershire to win matches, I was accepted without question by the senior players, many of whom went out of their way to encourage me and help me get through my first full season.

Although he was often away on Test duty, it was also a privilege to play in the same team as Gower who, at his best, was a simply sublime talent with a bat in his hands. Likewise with Willey – he was regarded by many people as a bowler but he was also capable of turning a match on its head with the bat.

You can't help but learn from being around players of that quality. I made my maiden century and had several match-winning contributions with the willow. Nevertheless, it didn't enter my head for one moment that I would be picked by England. It was an ambition, of course it was, but I was only 20 years of age, and was coming to the end of my first full season on the county circuit.

One of my senior teammates was Chris Balderstone and he used to frequently drag me into the visitors' changing rooms and tell me to listen to what was being said when the conversation turned to cricket. "Only by listening to other people will you learn," he said.

I remember after playing one Sunday League match we ended up in a pub afterwards. In those days it was common to get close to the fans and chat to them, and it was a part of the game that I loved. It is rather sad that contact is no longer part of the game. Apart from anything else, it gave us an opportunity to tell them about things that were happening that they might not otherwise have been aware of.

Chris asked me what I wanted to drink. "I will have a lager please."

"A pint or a half?"

"A pint."

"No you're not. "

"I want a pint."

"No, you're not having one."

"Why not?"

"You are having a half."

He then took me to one side and whispered: "Now listen Phil, you can have as many half pints as you want. The reason I bought you a half is because it looks better to the fans who come in here to see you with a half-pint glass in your hand rather than a pint. You can have 10 half-pints if you want."

And do you know what? He was right. If we had been seen knocking back pints of lager it would have created entirely the wrong impression. It was another lesson learnt. It was a piece of advice I never forgot, and I now pass it on to young cricketers. You don't go on courses to learn stuff like that.

I may not have known much at that time in my life, but I knew that there was a world of difference between county cricket and Test cricket.

During the winter of 1986, England was to tour Australia in another battle for the Ashes. Still fresh in the minds of most Englishmen were Ian Botham's heroics during the 1981 series. Everybody talks about Headingley, when he turned a hopeless situation into a winning one, but he made several other crucial contributions in that series with both bat and ball.

It was always said at the time that when Botham came out to bat, the bar would empty immediately because people wanted to see what he was going to do. Would he make another match-winning ton, would he make a quickfire fifty or would he be out quickly? No matter what the outcome, you always knew that you were going to be entertained when Beefy was at the crease.

It was the same with his bowling. He had that wonderful knack of being able to take a crucial wicket during the first over of a spell, sometimes at the start of a match, other times when England were struggling and desperately needed him to remove a star batsman. Or he could bowl like a drain for a few overs, take a wicket and go on to add four more in quick succession.

I loved watching him and dreamt that someday I might also play for England. As a fellow all-rounder, maybe I, too, could make the same sort of contribution that he did. And if I was incredibly lucky, maybe, just maybe, I might get to play alongside him.

Sometimes, you should be careful what you wish for...

People kept telling me that I might get a call-up to join the England party to go to Australia, even if it was only to get a bit of experience, but I dismissed it. Apart from anything else, I didn't know how big the Ashes series was. Yes, I was a cricketer and I had been a cricket fan, but I knew nothing of the history of the game or of the great rivalries that existed within the sport – England and Australia, Pakistan and India, Australia and New Zealand. As far as I was concerned, they just came together every so often and played a few Tests against one another.

When the county season finished I went out with a few of my teammates to celebrate. I was feeling pretty pleased with myself and felt that I deserved to let my hair down. The following day I was playing in a six-a-side benefit game at Grace Road for Paddy Cliffe. I remember walking into the ground nursing a hangover and really not feeling too good and the gate man, a tremendous character called Arthur, said: "Congratulations Phil."

I presumed he was congratulating me on the season I'd just had and I replied: "Thanks Arthur, that's good of you." As I turned to walk away, he said: "Aren't you excited?"

"Yes, it's been a great season. Cheers Arthur."

"No, no, no. I am not talking about that."

"Well what are you talking about then?"

"You've been selected to play for England on the winter tour of Australia."

"Stop messing around."

"Phil, I am serious. You have been chosen. There are TV crews waiting inside the ground for you."

"Yeah, yeah, yeah..."

I didn't believe him and carried on but when I got inside and saw all the TV crews, the penny suddenly dropped. He hadn't been pulling my leg. What you have to bear in mind is that this was a time before mobile phones – I believe that players now receive a text to tell them they have been selected.

Everybody was slapping me on the back and telling me how well I had done, how much I deserved it and what an incredible experience it would be for me. I then did a series of newspaper, television and radio interviews, but still the enormity of it all really hadn't sunk in. Here I was, at 20 years of age, in the England party to play the mighty Australians on their home turf. To be fair, it was a huge amount to take in. Oh yes, and at some point it registered with me that I would be paid about £10,000 for the tour – or, five times what I had earned for a full season with my county. For a young guy living in digs in Leicester, it seemed like a fortune.

All I had ever wanted to do was to become a professional cricketer, and I had done that. As far as I had been concerned, next on my agenda was the domestic season of 1987. But my life was about to change forever.

Eventually I got an official phone call, followed by a letter, and I suppose that was when I realised it was actually happening, that it hadn't been a dream or some elaborate wind-up. I joined the tour party at a hotel near Heathrow airport the day before we were due to fly out. There was lots of media work to do and I also had to pick up my official England kit – what a moment that was. It was something I had always hoped that I might have achieved at some point in my career, but at the age of 20? It seemed too good to be true.

At one point I looked in the bar and there were Ian Botham, David Gower and Allan Lamb, three of my heroes, sitting having a drink. I had to pinch myself. A lot of the players also had their families with them because the following day they were heading off and would be away from home for weeks.

It felt totally alien to me. I didn't feel that I belonged here and had problems grasping what was happening to me. Soon afterwards we all went for our kit and ended up back in the hotel bar together. We had to be up bright and early the next day but I knew that I would have problems sleeping because I was so excited and so nervous, so I went to bed late.

The following morning we had more press work to do, then we all got into our team kit and headed for the airport, where we were taken straight through to the first class lounge – this was another alien experience for me, something I had never experienced before. But it made sense. If the players had had to wait with everybody else, there would have been a constant demand for autographs.

One of the first things that struck me was that Botham and Lamb, who had been on the sauce the night before, picked up where they left off. Bearing in mind that we had a marathon flight ahead of us, I thought it seemed an odd thing to do, but they were happy and nobody seemed too bothered.

When an England team goes on tour now, there is a team manager, batting coach, bowling coach, fitness coach, masseur, chef, Uncle Tom Cobley and all. Back then, the party consisted of the players, Peter Lush, the team manager, and Mickey Stewart, the coach, and that was about it. Mind you, Stewart had only just taken over as coach, and he was about to put a rocket up the backsides of the players – something that didn't go down too well with some of the more senior members of the squad.

This was a fairly successful side, and Stewart was yet to make his presence felt.

I watched Beefy and Lamby downing their drinks and reached the conclusion that we were on some sort of a jolly.

Finally our flight was called and I found myself sitting next to Graham Dilley, the fast bowler. Botham and Lamb were still drinking as Dilley said to me: "Don't look at this tour as something where you will only be 12th man, just bringing drinks out to the middle. If you practice well, work hard and do well in the warm-up games you just never know, you might get in the team."

I was chuffed that a senior player should take the time to offer me such good advice. We settled into the flight, had something to eat and watched a movie, but whenever anybody tried to fall asleep, Botham and Lamb would wake us up – they weren't having any of it. By now, of course, they were both absolutely hammered. Naturally, it was the younger players they really picked on, the likes of my Leicestershire teammate James Whitaker, who was also on his first tour, and fast bowler Gladstone Small.

I thought it was funny. Some people get nasty with drink, but my two heroes were just having a laugh and were determined that everybody else would do too. But Dilley was becoming quite frustrated by it all. "I wish those two would just fall asleep so that the rest of us can get some peace and quiet."

At one point we landed in Singapore, and Botham and Lamb headed straight for the bar. I was surprised that the cabin crew let them back onto the plane but then we were off again and, unbelievably, the pair of them continued drinking throughout the flight.

About an hour or so before we landed in Brisbane, we were told to change out of our tracksuits and into slacks, blazer, shirt and tie – and that was the signal for them both to finally fall asleep.

We duly landed and, to my utter astonishment, Botham and Lamb woke up and got off the plane looking as if they hadn't touched a drop of alcohol for weeks. They got through a whole series of interviews with the Australian media without slurring their words or stumbling over their answers. I could not believe what I was witnessing. It was as remarkable a performance as anything they produced on the pitch in the weeks that were to follow.

I had been warned to expect sledging from the Australian cricketers – they would chip away with a series of verbals, hoping that they would hit a raw nerve. In a way, the sledging began the moment we arrived because the first advertising hoarding I saw depicted a kangaroo punching a lion. 'Pommie bashing' is part of the way of life in Australia and the locals are not at all embarrassed about shouting insults at members of a touring England cricket team.

We climbed on the team bus and arrived at the hotel and I hung back as I hadn't a clue what the protocol was.

Lush was busy sorting out the rooms and deciding who would stay with whom – I believe that a lot of players ask for their own rooms now, but back in the day we all had to share with one another. I figured I would probably end up rooming with James Whitaker or Graham Dilley. Then

Botham shouted over: "Right Phil, get your bags and follow me."

I was thinking: "What's going on? Why does he want me to go with him?" It briefly crossed my mind that perhaps I was going to be subjected to some initiation ceremony or other. But no, it was worse than that. "You are rooming with me," he announced.

I was numb and didn't know what to say. Beefy was my hero. I had watched him drink an aircraft dry, and now I was sharing a room with him. Only six months earlier, I wasn't even sure of a regular place in the Leicestershire team.

Before we headed towards our room, Mickey Stewart and Mike Gatting, the captain, had told everybody to put on shorts and a t-shirt because they wanted us to stay awake and go for a round of golf. We were all shattered and wanted to sleep, but Stewart and Gatts insisted that it would be better to stay awake and try to acclimatise to the time difference as quickly as possible. If we went to sleep right there and then, we wouldn't sleep at night-time and our body clocks would be all over the place.

We got to our room and I started to look for a pair of shorts. Meanwhile, Botham closed the curtains.

"What are you doing Ian? We are supposed to be going to play golf."

"Well you are playing golf, I am going to sleep, so get what you need and get out of here."

I grabbed my gear and went downstairs and told Mickey and Gatts that Botham had no intention of playing golf, but they were not surprised. That was when I first realised that Beefy played by his own rules and that he was, in many ways, a law unto himself. But if you have a genius in your ranks, a man who can win you games almost on his own, then you make some allowances. You just better make sure that if you are the genius in question that you carry on producing the goods because the moment you stop doing so, you are likely to find yourself out on your ear.

Mickey and Gatts knew that if they let the likes of Botham do things his own way, then they were likely to get the best out of him. I know that he would never get away with it today, and perhaps if he had been more disciplined then he might have been an even better cricketer, but you have to remember that we are talking about a man who could turn a match on its head single-handed.

It was my first experience of being in the company of such a huge star and I thought that the coach and captain got their man-management tactics absolutely spot on with Botham.

I played golf with Gatting and Dilley and we got back to the hotel at around 7pm. Gatts said that we would all eat together, so I went back to the room and opened the door as quietly as possible and heard: "Is that you?"

"Yes Ian, sorry if I woke you."

"What time is it?"

"Just after 7pm."

"Right then, time to get up."

"We are all meeting downstairs for something to eat."

"Well you are going downstairs for something to eat. I am going out with my manager."

So we both got washed and changed and I wandered down to the restaurant and told them Beefy was going out with his manager. Nobody seemed to be too surprised.

By the time it got to about 10pm I was absolutely shattered so I went back to the room and went to bed, looking forward to a peaceful night's sleep. Some chance!

At 2am the door crashed open and I woke up immediately. There in front of me was Ian Botham, holding a bottle of whisky and two glasses.

"Right then son, you are on tour. Pour."

I poured two glasses of whisky and that is the last thing I remember. I woke up the following morning and looked around the room. Botham was snoring his head off, and the bottle of whisky and two glasses were still there, untouched.

I woke him up and told him it was time to get up, and I jumped into the shower first. We both went down for breakfast and then picked up our kit before getting on a coach for a practice session. I sat next to Mike Gatting and said: "You will never believe what happened to me last night. Botham arrived back at the room with a bottle of whisky and told me to pour two glasses, but I didn't drink any of it, and the next thing I knew I fell asleep."

"Well you have passed your first test Phil because if you had touched a drop of that whisky he would have made you drink the whole bottle, so you did bloody well to crash out. Beefy doesn't like drinking on his own – trust me, you would have ended up absolutely hammered."

We then had a good practice session and I would have defied anybody to look at Botham and know he had been out on the lash the night before. And to be fair to him, he took me under his wing and looked after me. This was a guy I had worshipped and here he was showing an interest in me and my career. It was awesome, and it helped me to feel a part of the side.

The two of us roomed together for the next two weeks and during that time we had a lot of fun together but worked hard when we had to. I remember thinking to myself: "My God, this guy is a living legend, a *Boy's Own* hero, and now we are mates. How did that happen to me?" I was walking on air.

After two weeks, the management decided to change the room pairings and I was really disappointed. I didn't want to change. So who did they put me in with next? Allan Lamb. If you know anything about cricket of that vintage then you will not need me to tell you that Lamb was simply another version of Botham, which I guess is why the two of them got on so well together. I always loved the way these guys could have fun, but the minute they stepped out onto the pitch, everything became deadly serious. Lamb may have been born in South Africa but he was really proud to represent England and score runs for his teammates.

Lamb always had his music blaring away and, like Botham, he wanted to enjoy himself and have a few drinks, but he immediately stepped into Beefy's shoes and went out of his way to look after me. I was the new boy, the youngest member of the tour party, and these guys didn't want me to feel intimidated or overawed by it all. They could have just left me to it, to sink or swim on my own, but they didn't, and I will always feel grateful to them for that.

So I then had two weeks of sharing a room with Lamb. At that time, I was sponsored by Slazenger and so was he. I wasn't especially happy with the bat they had provided me with, but Lamby took control of that too. "Don't worry Phil, we'll call them and get it sorted for you."

Not only did he get me a new bat that I was happy with, but he also made sure I was given new pads and gloves – it was like Christmas. Throughout the tour they were like father figures to me. It was brilliant, and I could not have asked for more.

Just as I was getting comfortable with my roommate, I had to change again. I suppose it was done to ensure that cliques did not form within the tour party, and it did make a lot of sense, but it was difficult for me, a young lad on his first tour abroad with some of the greatest cricketers on the face of the earth. Bet you can't guess who was up next for me? A certain David Gower.

So I had gone from sharing with the team's two party animals to being with a man who was very quiet, well-spoken and extremely polite. He was a pretty chilled-out character who would sit and read a book and not say a great deal. I found it quite hard to talk to him because he was my county captain and I had a huge amount of respect for him.

The truth is that, to me, David was like a god, somebody I had placed on a pedestal and I could hardly talk to him. I just didn't know what to say to him because at that time in my life my conversational ability was rubbish so it reached the stage where I only spoke when he talked to me first or asked me a question. I was totally tongue-tied in his company, even more so than when I first met Beefy.

And did I mention that he also possessed the most sublime talent with a cricket bat in his hands?

My two weeks in a room with him were hard, and not very enjoyable, but it had nothing to do with him. It was all down to me. What could I say to this genius batsman that he would want to hear?

One night we went to a function in Bundaberg, Queensland, attended by a host of civic officials. To be frank, it was a pretty boring event, but then Gower, Beefy and Lamby came up with a way of livening things up. You may or may not know that Bundaberg is famous for producing rum – really strong rum – and our heroes decided that it might be fun to have a rum drinking contest. They started knocking this stuff back and the rest of us waited for the consequences.

When we got on the coach to go back to our hotel, Lamby and Botham were like a couple of naughty schoolboys, full of mischief, wanting to whack everybody and tell jokes. Gower, however, was rather quieter, right up to the point where he pushed open a window and hung out of it to be sick all over the road. As we were driving past a branch of Pizza Hut, Lamby told the driver to stop because he wanted to get out and buy himself a pizza, which he duly brought back onto the coach.

I looked around the bus – Gower was still hanging out the window, looking and feeling absolutely awful, Lamb was tucking into his pizza and Botham was acting the clown. This was the England cricket team on tour, and I was part of it. What's more, I was proud to be part of it.

Once more, Gatting and Stewart went along with it all. They were happy, just as long as things didn't get out of hand. And, by and large, everybody knew where to draw the line. You have to remember these were young men in the prime of their lives, away from home for weeks at a time. It was only natural that a few of them would want to let off steam.

Back in those days, there were a lot more warm-up games than the Test side plays now and we really weren't doing terribly well in those matches. It did occur to me that maybe there were some players who weren't quite giving 100%, but we were all having such a great time together and the atmosphere in the changing room was so good that nobody seemed to be too bothered.

Before I tell you about the rest of the tour or any more about my life and career, you should know something about my childhood, which shaped the person I am today.

CHAPTER 2:
GROWING PAINS

Although I consider myself to be British, I was actually born in Scotts Head, Dominica, which is between Martinique and Guadeloupe, on 18 February, 1966. I was christened Phillip Anthony Jason DeFreitas.

My grandfather, Thomas DeFreitas, was Portuguese. He studied law in Guyana, where my father, Martin, who was one of four brothers, was educated.

Grandfather owned a big estate in Scotts Head and when he died, the land was split between his four sons. Martin met and married my mother, Sybil, who is half French and half Dominican, and they moved into a house on the estate. They would eventually have seven sons.

I don't have too many memories of Dominica but those I do have are all good and mostly revolve around playing in the sea with my friends and brothers. I didn't play any cricket, or any other sport for that matter, although my brothers did. Let me introduce them to you. Roland, Richie, Roy, Faron, Reuben and Simeon. I was number five.

My older brothers played a bit of cricket but I had no interest in sport whatsoever. I used to just run around throwing stones.

School was tough, very tough, and the teachers were very strict. I was quite lively, although no more than anybody else, and I remember being caned fairly often. It was a combination of me misbehaving and the teachers being sadists, and the worst thing of all was that we would be told to go and choose the cane with which we were going to be punished.

When we turned up for school in the morning, our nails, ears and hair were checked to make sure we were clean. I didn't have a problem with that, and have been pretty fastidious about my personal hygiene ever since. Most schoolchildren in the Caribbean are smartly dressed, no matter how poor the background they might be from – it teaches you disciplines that stay with you for the rest of your life, and that can never be a bad thing.

Mum and Dad decided they were going to live in England, but they couldn't afford to take Reuben and me, so they initially left us behind with my grandmother, Matilda, who owned a shop in Scotts Head. Apart from anything else, my parents thought it best that Reuben and I continued to attend school in Dominica.

In the end, we were with my grandmother for five years and I desperately missed my parents, especially my Mum. Even though they came back to see us a few times, I felt lost, abandoned even. My grandmother was a terrific lady but she wasn't my Mum. I guess Reuben and I just felt alone in the world.

Eventually the day came when my parents had saved enough money to pay for airline tickets and they sent for us to join them in London. We were taken on a two-hour car drive from Scotts Head to a place called Roseau, and it was a horrendous drive along some really dangerous roads and at the end of the journey was Melville Hall airport. I was nine years old and was travelling alone with my brother to England, so the two of us were put in a room because they didn't want us wandering around the airport. I was scared, even though I knew that at the end of it all, we were going to see our parents and brothers again.

Finally we got on a plane that took us to Antigua, where we were put in another room for two or three hours. Then there was another plane. It was huge and Reuben and I were genuinely scared, but we were escorted on board and the next thing we knew was that we were landing in England and suddenly I was freezing my rocks off and thinking: "What is this place?" I was from Dominica – I had no idea what it was to feel cold, but I learnt pretty damn quickly because this was January and it was winter. Welcome to England!

My father picked us up and gave us each an apple – it was the first time in my life I had ever seen an apple, let alone eaten one. As we drove, I looked around at this new world I was expected to live in and it all felt totally alien to me. I wanted to go home. I certainly didn't want to feel cold. My father told us it was a different life and there wouldn't be any running around because there wasn't enough room in the flat, and Reuben started to cry.

Home was Harlesden in north London, not Scotts Head in Dominica. And they were living in a flat. So here we were, seven boys and my Mum and Dad, living in a flat. Dad said that he emigrated because he wanted to give his family a better life, but nine people in a flat hardly seemed like a better life, even to me as a naïve nine-year-old boy.

I was happy to be reunited with my brothers, but was shocked by where we were living and by the weather. I had no idea it was going to be like this. Simeon, the youngest of the DeFreitas clan, had been born since Mum and Dad had moved to England, so I was seeing him for the first time and he was already a year old.

There were two or three of us sharing a bed. It just didn't feel right to me and I quickly became homesick. Back in Dominica we had shared rooms but our house was much bigger than this flat, and we all had space. Here, it was claustrophobic and it didn't seem like a better life to me.

Harlesden was a shock to my system, just as it was to my brothers. It didn't help that my father drank a lot and he was aggressive when he had been drinking so growing up around him was not a barrel of laughs. He was aggressive towards my Mum and towards us boys, and I was scared of him. I used to hide whenever I heard Country and Western music being played because that was always the signal that he was drinking.

First of all he would start to get louder and louder, and then the aggression would begin. I say that I used to hide but the truth is that in a flat such as the one we lived in there was nowhere to hide but we used to shut ourselves in the bedroom, afraid that he would come in and lose his temper with us.

My father's behaviour had a profound effect on me. Having been taken away from my proper home, where I didn't have a care in the world other than perhaps upsetting one of my teachers and being caned as a result, I felt that there was now no enjoyment in my life. I didn't want to be around my Dad, and I think most of my brothers felt exactly the same way.

One of the things you need to know about families from the West Indies is that they are incredibly together and loyal towards one another, and I am sure that one of the main reasons that my older brothers stayed when they could have left and found somewhere of their own to live was that they wanted to look after my Mum and make sure she didn't come to any harm.

In effect, they sacrificed their careers. My older brothers played cricket and football with Mike Gatting and he told me that they were highly talented at both, but they didn't take things any further because they wanted to protect their mother.

And I also believe that they gave up on any dreams they might have had for my benefit. Without them being there, I am not quite sure how things would have panned out, but they always were there for me.

Dad had always enjoyed a drink but it definitely got worse when he came to England. He worked for the Post Office, but every Friday he would get paid and he would be drunk when he got home and he would put the dreaded Country and Western music on and open a bottle of whisky – when that was gone, one of the boys would be sent out to get some more. Then the music would get louder and louder.

The funny thing is that for all that hearing Country and Western music represented my father being drunk, I did learn to love it and if I ever hear it on the radio now I don't mind listening to it.

My Mum put up with this behaviour because she loved him and was and remains a devout Roman Catholic. You also have to take into account the fact that she had seven sons and looking after us was a full-time job, so she couldn't go out and work, and that in turn meant that she had no real independence. She was utterly dependent on my father for everything. We are also talking about a generation who, when they got married, did so for life, for 'better or for worse'.

Dad felt he was the best at everything he did or had done, and he was a man who always wanted to be in control, who had to be in charge of everything.

The way that he was towards my mother and us boys had a deep impact on me. I have already admitted that I was frightened of him, but I also had no love for him as I grew up. I was an unhappy child, and not just because of my Dad.

In Scotts Head, we spoke English, but we also spoke in broken French, patois as it is called. When I came to London I attended Oldfield Primary School and I really struggled in all sorts of ways and just didn't want to be there. I was like a fish out of water. Everything was strange to me and I withdrew into my shell and became very shy and quiet.

The result of this was that I guess I must have been pretty hard work for my teachers, but rather than recognising that I was so quiet because I was unhappy, I guess they came to the conclusion that I was just plain awkward. One day an exasperated teacher belted me with a book. I cried all the way home, told Dad what had happened and he came to the school the next day, but fortunately he didn't make a huge scene.

I somehow managed to get through it all and then went to Willesden High School. You won't be surprised to learn that I had been dreading going to what was a bigger school, although I did think that it might be even easier for me to hide away there and continue to be anonymous.

But then one day I was in a French lesson and, much to my surprise, I found that I was really enjoying it because I could understand the language and it gave me an edge on my classmates, the first time anything like that had occurred since I had arrived in England. Suddenly, I had found something I could excel at.

That didn't last long though. One day I was asked if I could play any musical instruments. Back in Dominica I had played a bit of guitar but, without thinking, I replied in the broken French version I had learnt growing up: "Gita." A couple of boys in the class fell about laughing. They laughed and laughed. It had the effect of sending me back into my shell again. I was embarrassed and I was afraid at one and the same time. I told the teacher that I needed to go to the toilet and I locked myself in a cubicle and cried for an hour.

Life at Willesden should have been good for me because it was about a 50-50 split between black and white kids. I continued to struggle though until, finally, sport came along and saved me.

I had never played football before but it was the main sport at school, and during the winter it was really the only sport. I discovered that I enjoyed it and, better than that, I was pretty good at it, good enough to be chosen to play for the school.

Faron played a bit of cricket for Sudbury Court during the summer. At first I used to go along and watch him, but then he encouraged me to have a go and I discovered that I had a knack for it and soon found myself playing club cricket for Sudbury Court. I also played cricket for the school.

So now I had sport as an outlet, something that I could look forward to and enjoy. I still didn't enjoy the academic side of school and hated going to lessons, with the exception of French. I was also bullied mentally – I figure that I could have handled it had the bullying been physical because I could have fought back, but mental bullying is the worst kind of bullying, where people constantly put you down or make fun of you just because of the way you speak, or whatever. Eventually it had such a profound effect on me that I even stopped enjoying the French lessons, to the point where I somehow managed to forget everything I had known about the language from back home in Dominica. I just blanked it out. In truth, I was a pretty complex kid and was badly mixed up.

There was a girl who sat behind me in class and back in those days I had quite long hair, and she started to pull it. Day after day it went on. I asked her to stop, but she continued doing it. It was almost as if she was trying to see how far she could push me. Finally, I'd had enough and I turned round and shouted at her, making it perfectly clear that she'd better stop.

A day or so later, I was walking out of class and the girl's boyfriend walked up to me in the corridor and head-butted me. There was no warning, nothing was said. But the funny thing is, I could cope with that. It was the mental stuff that really got me down.

On another occasion I was in class and wasn't paying attention. I wasn't being malicious or anything like that. It was just one of those things. I was actually writing down my cricket team for a match we were playing that Saturday and the teacher realised I was lost in my own world and asked me a question. "Sorry sir," I said, figuring there was no point in being anything other than totally honest, "but I have no idea."

He called me to the front of the class and asked me what I had been doing. Again, it seemed foolish to make up a story so I told him the truth, that I had been picking my cricket team.

What are you going to do when you leave school DeFreitas?" he asked.

"I'm going to be a cricketer."

Everybody laughed out loud. It is impossible for me to properly explain how that made me feel, but as I returned to my desk I felt really small and utterly humiliated. My classmates were not only laughing, but they were making jokes at my expense. The upshot was that I stopped going to lessons taught by that teacher because I couldn't face him or the kids, so I decided to avoid it.

They say that you remember your good teachers for the rest of your life. All I can say is that I don't remember too many of them – not for the right reasons at any rate. Good teachers identify the kids who need help. It is all too easy to use the size of a class as an excuse and to turn a blind eye, but I felt that was what happened to me. I needed emotional support and nobody recognised that. I wasn't strong enough to ask for help but the truth is that I felt my teachers were part of the problem. Things weren't good at home either, so I couldn't find the answers there either.

Sport was the only thing that motivated me and I used to bunk off school all the time and would spend my days in the park, or I would kick a football around or sometimes I would take a tennis ball and throw it against a wall and catch it; anything to keep my mind off school. What I used to do was roll up to school in the morning, attend registration and then disappear for the day.

Of course I was caught many times, and letters would be sent to my parents. Mum worried constantly about me and Dad used to get very angry with me but as frightened as I was of the consequences, I was prepared to risk facing them rather than going to school.

The times when I did go to school I would sit in the corner of the classroom and not talk to anybody. I soon found myself in a classic Catch-22 situation – because I was missing so much schooling I was falling further and further behind everybody else, and that just made me all the more determined not to go in because I was struggling so terribly and becoming more and more withdrawn.

Then I was put into a remedial class, and you can guess what that was like, I am sure. I was with kids who really were troublemakers and I got mixed up with them and found myself hating school even more. I just didn't realise how important education was.

Each morning I would wake up and have these feelings of dread about going into school. I would tell Mum how I felt but she would always say the same thing. "You need to go to school, you need to get an education."

She wanted me to become a doctor or a lawyer, and I found it very difficult to explain to her exactly how I felt. I was able to tell her I didn't enjoy it, but I wasn't able to talk to her about the mental bullying, the fact that I was struggling with lessons or anything like that. Perhaps if I had been able to have that discussion then things might have been very different. As for my father, well I could hardly say anything to him, far less try to tell him the way I felt about my schooling.

I avoided my father whenever I could and it got to the stage, that if he was out of the house, I was happy. As soon as he came home, I felt frightened and depressed. Talking about it now, it sounds terrible, but that's the way it was. And when he came home I would try to find any excuse to get out of the house.

I confided in a teacher called Ellis Williams, a Welshman who had played rugby: "I love my cricket and my football but I am really struggling in my lessons Mr Williams, not because I am stupid but because I suppose that I am scared to open my mouth. I sit in a lesson and my mind goes blank." He was horrified.

I had a couple of friends, but that was through my football and cricket. There was a guy called Glenroy Mundell and another called Harry Nembard – we played football together for the school and in a Sunday League and, as a result, we kind of hung out together. Chris Lewis, who went on to become an England cricketer, went to my school. He was two years below me.

It was through club cricket, however, that I made what I would call real friends. After a time I came to regard Sudbury Court as my family because we all had the same interests in common and I was treated as an equal and wasn't subjected to any taunting or mental bullying. I was comfortable in that environment.

They also had a rugby club and the guys who played that were really sociable too, and I ended up working behind the bar washing and drying the glasses in order to make a little bit of pin money. It gave me a small piece of independence and I slowly began to find an identity. That joyless life I spoke about earlier began to have some purpose, and I finally had something to look forward to.

I was also named as captain of my school cricket team, which played on Saturdays. Next up for me should have been the London schools team and Middlesex Colts, but I didn't get anywhere close to being chosen for those, and everybody kept telling me it was because I was going to the 'wrong' school, and that if I had been attending a private school then I would have walked in. There should also have been the England schools team, but you have already guessed, and you are quite correct. I didn't get a look-in. I kept thinking how strange it was that I wasn't being selected for these teams because everybody knew that I was a decent cricketer.

I was selected to play for Middlesex Schools, and my first match for them was against North Yorkshire. We played another Middlesex Schools match at Evershed's ground in London and I had to catch a bus to get to the ground. My Mum gave me 50p and I had my kit in a plastic bag, something that was to become a feature of my early days in the game. I didn't even have a packed lunch with me. As I got to the ground, the other players were being dropped off by their parents, and they were all wearing blazers, shirts and ties. I felt a bit like Alf Tucker, from *The Beano*.

For all that cricket had given me new-found confidence, as I sat in the dressing room that day and watched all these smartly-dressed, intelligent boys walk in, I considered standing up, walking out and heading straight home because I felt like a fish out of water again. It was a horrible feeling, a sense of not belonging.

For some reason, I decided not to go. There was a boy sitting next to me – I have no idea what his name was, but I hope with all my heart that he reads this book – and he went out of his way to talk to me, to be friendly towards me. I felt relaxed again and we went out and bowled and I got into a great rhythm and got up a good head of steam and took six wickets. We then headed back to the dressing room and everybody was really happy. They all started to take their lunch boxes out and there I was with nothing, not even so much as a piece of fruit or a packet of sweets.

The boy who had spoken to me earlier was sitting beside me again. "Where's your lunch?" he asked.

"I haven't got any."

"Well in that case you can share mine."

And so it was that he gave me a couple of his salad sandwiches and chatted away to me. We ended up winning the match and at the end of it all I felt brilliant. But then, at the end of the game, all the parents came in their cars to pick up the other boys, while I grabbed my plastic bag and set off for the bus home.

While I loved playing cricket, especially for Sudbury Court, I used to dread going home. It sounds terrible, I know it does, but that was how I felt. If I had played well, Dad would always find a way of deflating me. I would come through the front door and say to him: "I played really well today."

"You are not a cricketer, your brother is," he would reply.

When your confidence is already fairly fragile, that sort of thing can only make you feel worse. It was like I was constantly being put down. Needless to say, he never came along to watch me play in those club matches. I found myself wishing that he didn't exist. I was embarrassed by him, I was embarrassed by my feelings for him and I was embarrassed by our circumstances in terms of where we were living and what we had left behind.

Not surprisingly, I got into a few scrapes and fights during those days but, fortunately, nothing too serious. There was one occasion where a lad who had been taunting me just said one thing too much and I thumped him – he hit me back and we rolled around for a while and then I realised I had lost a tooth, so when I got home I told my Mum that I had fallen over in the playground, which was kind of true. There were other times when I wanted to lash out, but I restrained myself. I knew that although my brothers were on the scene, I had to learn to look out for myself because I believed that nobody else would, but fighting wasn't the answer.

I have always been, and still am, a calm and relaxed person who believes that violence and conflict solves nothing – it simply creates more violence and conflict.

The ironic thing was that through hanging around with the boys from the remedial class, I found that I suddenly had some street cred, for no reason other than the fact that I was prepared to play truant. How crazy was that?

I hated exams but eventually the time came to sit my O-levels and I knew that there was no hiding place for me. Surprisingly, some of my grades were okay but I remember walking into the hall to do my history exam and I put my name and class at the top of the paper, looked at the questions and decided to walk out there and then. There were repercussions, with the school informing my parents what I had done, but I just told them that I was scared, an emotion which was a recurring theme throughout my teenage years.

It wasn't because I was afraid of the actual history exam, because I knew the majority of the answers and could have passed but I looked around and there were certain people sitting close to me who intimidated me, and I knew that I couldn't face the exam. Sadly, I never did get the chance to take it again.

When my O-levels were over there was only one thing for me to do, and that was to leave school, with the intention of perhaps coming back at some stage to retake some of the exams I hadn't done well in, along with the history test. It never happened though.

CHAPTER 3
FALTERING STEPS

I left school with a handful of O-levels and the knowledge that I was a decent footballer and cricketer, but not the first idea what I was going to do with the rest of my life. Charlie Myers, my captain at Sudbury Court, wrote to the MCC on my behalf, told them that he believed I was a very promising cricketer and that I would fit right in as a member of the Lord's groundstaff.

I was invited to a trial along with another hundred boys and turned up in jeans, which seemed entirely natural to me, and I had to borrow a pair of cricket boots from a member of Sudbury Court's cricket team – they were ancient. I didn't have boots of my own; I played in trainers. I also took club pads, a club bat and club gloves. God alone knows what I must have looked like, but in the end, I drew the line at the boots and ended up having my trial in my trainers. Everybody else turned up with a proper kit bag; I had a plastic bag. Everybody else was driven to Lord's in posh cars; I got the bus.

During the trial I had to show what I could do with bat and ball. Before I go any further, I should explain what it means to be a member of the MCC groundstaff. If you do well enough at the trial to be offered a position, it effectively means that you are being taken on as a young professional cricketer. There are, of course, absolutely no guarantees that it will come to anything, but it is a start, it is a chance to follow your dream.

The MCC coach at the time was a man called Don Wilson and one of the players I attended my trial with was a young spin bowler you may also have heard of – his name was Phil Tufnell, aka The Cat – not because he was lithe like a cat but because he could sleep anywhere, and I do mean anywhere.

Anyway, Tufnell and I were told that we had been unsuccessful and that we were not going to be offered contracts. I was gutted, devastated. My feeling was that I had performed well enough during the trial, that there was nobody there who was better than me and that I was good enough to be selected. I was utterly deflated and as I left the ground all sorts of thoughts went through my head, chief among them being the idea that I hadn't been chosen because of the colour of my skin or that it was because I had attended Willesden High School. It may surprise you to learn that Tufnell attended private school – he was kicked out though, and I don't imagine that will come as a great shock.

Fortunately, Wilson had seen something in us and told the powers-that-be that he wanted both of us, so the decision was reversed and we received letters informing us that we were now in.

As elated as I was, I should make one thing clear here – being a junior member of the MCC groundstaff is just about the lowest of the low, and the money was awful. But it was a start, a foothold on a sport that I fancied I could make a living from.

By then, I was also playing football for Sudbury Court and the coach was sufficiently impressed with me to get me a couple of games with Luton Town's youth team. At that time, Luton Town had a decent football team. Three years earlier he had identified another Sudbury Court footballer as somebody with potential and arranged for him to have a trial with Watford. That player's name was John Barnes. Unfortunately, I was no John Barnes, and I knew it.

I was a central defender and I was comfortable on the ball. Later, I was told that Luton thought I was a decent player and they would have been prepared to offer me an apprenticeship but I had already made up my mind that I was going to take the MCC position and see if I could make it as a professional cricketer.

Sudbury Court used to practise one day a week at Lord's so I used to join them, and I discovered that I could get into the ground whenever I wanted just by saying I was with this person or that person, and they would let me in and I could practise and play until my heart's content. I would approach every team that turned up at Lord's and ask if I could bowl at their batsmen and ended up bowling non-stop to different sides from 6pm until 10pm. I couldn't get enough of it.

It was a train journey from Lord's to home and sometimes I didn't have my train fare so I used to sneak on and off, making sure that I never got caught. Or if I was lucky enough to have any lunch money, I would save it so that I could pay my train fare. Most young sportsmen from working-class backgrounds will tell similar stories – it is what you do because you love it so much and you just want to get better and better, whether it be cricket, football, tennis or golf.

I used to walk from home to Neasden station, which took about half an hour, and then get the train to St John's Wood, walk down to the ground and tell the guy on the gate: "Yeah, I am practising tonight." My friends used to laugh at me when I told them what I was doing, night after night, but I was comfortable doing it.

The best thing about getting on to the groundstaff was that I received a kit allowance so, for the first time in my life, I was able to get a new pair of bowling boots. Heaven! I felt that I had arrived. I also had my first bat, gloves, pads and helmet. At least I looked like a cricketer. I felt like I had died and gone to heaven.

A lot of the guys had come from other parts of the country and they also received an allowance to pay for hostel accommodation in Hampstead. Luxury it wasn't, but I suppose that the best thing about it was that it helped you to find out whether or not you really did want to be a cricketer. If you were prepared to put up with that kind of privation while learning your craft, then the chances were that you would put up with anything. And in that respect it was pretty clever.

I was officially still staying at home, but I hardly ever went home. I used to ask the lads if they minded me sleeping on their floors. Looking back, it probably wasn't the perfect preparation for somebody with designs on becoming a fast bowler because it did my back no good at all, but it meant that I was always around fellow cricketers, guys with the same dreams as mine; what's more, they were all setting out on the same path as me and we were all equals. The only thing that separated us was our ability to play cricket.

My parents used to worry, but at least they had some idea that I was all right.

If we were playing away from home then it was real luxury – we used to get put up in hotels.

Some of the guys used to go to the pub and I started going with them, desperately trying to scrape together enough money on my puny wage to buy a couple of pints of beer. It all helped me in my aim to stay away from home and out of the way of my father.

It was also while I was at MCC that I was called Daffy for the first time, and you probably won't be all that surprised to learn that it was Tufnell who came up with it. We were good mates and spent a lot of time together, and during fielding practice we used to mess around quite a lot. Some of you might be surprised to learn that Tuffers ever did fielding practice but I can assure you that he did.

During one session, the ball was hit, somebody shouted "Phil" and we both went for it and ended up rolling around on the grass together, at which point Don Wilson said: "You two really are daft. You do some daft things."

From that moment on, Tufnell christened me 'Daffy', although at times it became 'Daffodil', and whenever I played against Mark Ealham at Kent, he would say: "Here comes the Freight Train."

I felt it was kind of neat that people came to know me by my nickname. There are not many people who are instantly known by their nickname – Beefy, Athers, Bumble... For me, it was a sign that people had taken me to their hearts. Hardly anybody calls me Phil now, although I have never been too comfortable with complete strangers walking up to me and calling me 'Daffy'.

Tufnell and I had various duties that we had to perform at Lord's. Whenever the ground staged a Test, we either had to sell scorecards or look after the scoreboard. During one match we were sitting in a hut selling cards to the members and we quickly became bored, so we decided to put the cards on a table and sit back and relax, and as the members arrived we told them: "Help yourselves to a card, but just leave the money there."

We were reported to a Colonel Stevenson, who was in charge of us, and he warned us about our conduct, but the thing was that the colonel loved

Tuffers – everybody did. He also had a soft spot for me. Yes, he saw us as two characters, but he also saw us as two decent cricketers who might have a bright future.

Every time we were dragged in front of him he would tell us that it was our final warning.

We ended up looking after the scoreboard during a county game. I believe that Middlesex was playing Glamorgan, and there were three of us in the box – myself, Tuffers and a big lad called Tony. In those days, everything was operated by hand, and I was in charge of one part of the board, while Phil looked after another. Once again, we quickly grew bored – we just wanted to be outside playing cricket, not scoring it.

Every time a run was scored, Tuffers yanked at his part of the board as hard as he possibly could, with Tony, who had a quiet, squeaky voice, telling him to ease up. Phil paid no attention and continued to yank away at it until the inevitable happened, and it fell apart.

We were sent to see the colonel again. "What am I going to do with the pair of you?" he said. "Listen boys, and I am serious this time, this is your final warning."

Our punishment was to stay behind one night to perform an extra session bowling at MCC members who were coming in for a net. Once you have done a full day, the last thing you want is a net session with the members, but we had no choice. Some of them would hand over a fiver, £10 or a can of Coke, but it still wasn't much fun.

As Tufnell and I stood by the net, Colonel Stevenson appeared, bat in hand. He seemed very old to us back then but I suppose he would only have been about 50. He was a lovely man, but the two of us had a quick chat and decided to give him a good working over, with me bowling seamers at him and Tufnell bowling spin. Our theory was that we would never be asked to bowl at the members again.

I kept sending down bouncers and he knew exactly what we were up to, but he took it all in good heart and we never did have to bowl at the members again, so maybe we weren't quite as stupid as we looked.

The two of us were pretty lucky and missed out on a lot of the duties we should have been performing because we were regularly called up for either Middlesex Seconds or Under-25s. There was one match when we faced Leicestershire Seconds, whose team included Gordon Parsons and Jonathan Agnew. I was batting and Parsons was coming in at full steam and I managed to launch him into the ladies loo at long on at Grace Road. Agnew was in hysterics but when he bowled the next over at me I hit him for six over extra cover down the Milligan Road. I don't believe the ball was ever seen again.

CHAPTER 4
MAKING MY POINT

Having missed out on the representative cricket in and around London that I deserved to play, my profile was obviously a little bit higher through being on the MCC staff and playing various matches for them, and my first call-up came for the England Under-19 team. Phil Tufnell was also chosen, and off we went to the West Indies.

I couldn't believe it, and imagine going back to my roots for my first tour with England. You couldn't make it up. We went to Barbados, St Lucia and Jamaica, so there was no chance for me to catch up with family while I was out there, but it didn't matter. What did matter was that I was representing England in three Under-19 Test matches. Life surely didn't get any better than that.

Bob Willis was the tour manager and Bob Cottam was our coach, and I learnt a great deal from Willis in particular; he had been a terrific pace bowler for England and was a man who never gave less than 100%.

When we first arrived in Barbados we had been told not to drink the local rum because it was very, very strong. To a group of young lads, most of them away from home for the first time in their lives, that was like a red rag to a bull. Tufnell, myself and John Addison, who was at Leicestershire at the time, and Smudger Smith from Glamorgan decided that we were going to go out and buy some of this stuff and take it back to our room.

We started drinking it and before long we were all absolutely hammered. Normally, we would have got away with it but the problem was that on this particular night we had to attend a team dinner and all four of us were late – and drunk.

Willis and Cottam looked at us and one of them said: "I think you guys need some water."

Addison responded with: "Water? F****** water? You know what you can do with that."

We were immediately told to go back to our rooms and sober up.

I also learned another lesson on that trip. Early on, I pulled a side muscle and I was in pain for the whole time we were out there, but because I wanted to play so badly, I never really revealed the full extent of it. Because I kept playing, it didn't have a chance to heal and the result was that I didn't do myself justice on that tour. If I had asked to sit out the first Test, it might have been a different story, but remember that you are talking about somebody who, not long before this, had been turning up at Lord's every night to bowl solidly for four hours. The way I saw it, this was my big chance and I wasn't going to let it pass me by.

We lost the series against a West Indies side that included the likes of Carl Hooper and Jimmy Adams but it was a fun tour and I enjoyed it and felt that I grew up while I was away.

Two or three of the lads in the under-19 team were already playing county cricket, while Tuffers and I were still MCC groundstaff. At the start of the following summer I was travelling to a match with Mark Blackett, who joined at the same time as me, and we were heading off to play a Leicestershire second team. We were in Mark's car and I hadn't the foggiest idea where we were heading. We could have been going north, south, east or west and it would have meant nothing to me.

All that I knew was that we were travelling to Leicester, and all that I knew about Leicestershire was that this was the team the great David Gower played for, and he was one of my heroes. I was very naïve back in those days, so naïve that when we were driving into Leicester for the very first time, I looked around and saw a couple of blonde people and thought to myself: "Yes, this is Gower's town right enough."

For me, there was something extraordinary about the city of Leicester right from day one. Quite apart from the belief that everybody must be blonde, which I quickly realised was hokum, from that very first day I had this feeling that I belonged, that I was meant to be there. It is very difficult to explain, and I know that it must sound far-fetched, but I am sure that most people have nice, warm, fuzzy feelings about certain places, and I just knew that I was meant to be in Leicester the city and Leicestershire the county.

If you have ever had a sense of deja vu you will know how I felt when we drove through the gates of Grace Road, the Leicestershire county ground, for the first time.

I batted and bowled well and had a decent game and at the end of the day I was sitting in the changing rooms with a lovely feeling about the place when Ken Higgs, the Leicestershire coach, walked in and approached Andy Wagner, the MCC groundstaff coach, and told him that he wanted Mark Blackett and myself to play a couple of second-team games for Leicestershire.

I couldn't stop smiling. It was difficult to fathom and impossible to explain, but I just want to repeat it again so that there can be no mistake – I had arrived in the city and then at the ground and I had known with absolute certainty that this was a place I was meant to be, and now, at the end of a match on that same day, I was being offered the opportunity to return, with a view to joining the county. It was beyond belief.

My understanding was that a young cricketer spent two years on the groundstaff and if he was very lucky then he may be picked up by a county. But to be offered this chance halfway through my first year, well it simply didn't happen.

Mark and I duly went back to Leicestershire to play for the second team. I vividly remember my first game. James Whittaker, the first-team batsman, was in the side because he wanted some practice, and my early impressions were of an arrogant man. He didn't speak to us at all. It appeared to me that all he wanted to do was to bat for himself, score as many runs as possible and have no interest in anybody else. He was incredibly single-minded.

I would soon learn that he was actually a terrific bloke, and the two of us became close friends.

Mike Haysman, the captain, on the other hand, was somebody I connected with right from the off. That first match was a three-day affair against Worcestershire, who had Graeme Hick in their team, so there were some top quality players on show.

Before the game finished, Ken Higgs took me to one side and told me that Leicestershire wanted to offer me a two-year contract if I was interested. Interested? I nearly bit his hand off. He also offered Mark a contract. The two of us were simply overjoyed. This really was fantasy cricket, the best news ever.

So Mark and I then headed back to London to tell Don Wilson and the MCC groundstaff guys that we were heading north to further our careers. I had been playing Middlesex under-25 games and when

Middlesex were informed that I had been offered a contract at Grace Road, I was called in by Tim Lamb, the chief executive, and he told me: "Phil, we would like to offer you a contract, but we can't see you playing first-team cricket for a few years." At that time, Middlesex had Wayne Daniel, Norman Cowans, Neil Williams and Simon Hughes and in reserve they had Angus Fraser and Kevin James, so I was going to be way down the food chain.

If I'd had any doubts about moving to Leicestershire, they were dispelled in that instant, so I left the meeting and told Ken Higgs I would be joining him. I later discovered that Mike Gatting and John Emburey, two of Middlesex's England internationals, were extremely upset that I left, but it wasn't until I spoke to them some years later that they realised the circumstances and discovered what I had been told.

These were obviously two cricketers who saw something in me that perhaps others on the management side didn't.

For me, one of the critical factors in reaching my decision to move to Leicester was that here was a county who showed interest in me and who made it obvious that they cared about me, something I hadn't often felt in my life up to that point.

I guess that the most difficult thing was telling Mum that I was leaving home, but she knew that it was what I really wanted to do and that I would be happy. I also knew that if it didn't work out, I could always head back to London, although I was determined there was no way that was going to happen.

I wanted to get away, and when I had taken the decision it felt as if a huge burden had been lifted from my shoulders. By this stage, all my older brothers were living their own lives, doing their own thing.

You might be surprised to learn that it was only when I started my first season with Leicestershire that I finally decided to put any football dreams I still had on hold, as I knew that it was going to be well-nigh impossible to play both. There were exceptions of course – there always are. At Grace Road, we had an exceptional opener, Chris Balderstone, who also played football for Carlisle United; Ian Botham managed to play cricket and the occasional game for Scunthorpe United; and Phil Whitticase, another Leicestershire cricketer, played a few games for Birmingham City.

We used to play the occasional six-a-side football match and at one point Balderstone took me to one side and said: "You look like you can play a bit Phil. Why don't you play both?"

"To be honest Chris, I don't think I would be able to because I would be afraid of picking up injuries that would prevent me from playing cricket, and cricket is the game I really love."

He tried his best to persuade me, but I would not be moved. In general, the two sports just didn't mix. Besides, I wondered what the Leicestershire staff would say if I turned up and told them that I'd broken my ankle playing football! I think you can take it for granted that nobody would have been too impressed.

Besides, I could look back with pride on the fact that as a 15-year-old I had played for the senior team at Sudbury Court and I had also played for Luton. In fact, apart from the school, I played all my football at senior level as a teenager, and that was enough for me. Our school football kit was orange, just like Holland – not that we played like the Dutch though.

But when I signed my first professional cricket contract, I decided it was time to stop playing football. Much of it was down to Ellis Williams, my games teacher, who told me that if I wanted something then I should just focus on it and go for it, and I wanted to be the best cricketer I could be.

The support I received from Ellis really drove me on and made up for the fact that my own father didn't give me the backing he should have done. I am pretty certain that I am correct in saying that my father never once took me to a cricket or football match. The sense I had when I was growing up was that he didn't care, other than when it suited him.

Don't get me wrong – I am certain he was proud when he knew that I had been asked to play for Leicestershire, but he always found it difficult, if not impossible, to show his emotions. He was never the sort of man who would put his arms around me and tell me he loved me. I don't know why, but lots of men seem to be like that, so when somebody comes into your life who seems to show some genuine interest in you then it is pretty obvious you are going to gravitate towards that person.

The truth is that I always felt Dad had so much to offer. I have two young sons and he is brilliant with them, but we will return to that subject later.

Even before I moved to Leicester, I had switched off my own emotions towards the man who had brought me to England. From the age of 13 or 14 I felt nothing for him in terms of love and warmth and did my level best to have nothing to do with him. When he came in, I would go out. This is not an easy thing for me to address but I feel that I must if I am to give you a sense of who I am, what I have been through and what I have done with my life.

I felt pure hatred towards him because I felt he had let me down. More than anything else, I believed that he had let me down when it came to the education side of things because he was and is a very intelligent man, but he didn't pass any of his knowledge on to us or spend time helping us with homework or stressing how important it was to work hard at school. Yes, I should have known that hard work was required, but sometimes you need a parent to emphasise that.

He was selfish in that respect and when it was combined with the drinking and the aggression, it was more than enough for me to shut him out of my life. Although we were living under the same roof, I had effectively already cut all ties with Dad, so when I went to Leicester, it was easy to have nothing more to do with him.

My brothers told me that he watched me whenever I was on TV and that he would watch videos of me as my career progressed so he was clearly proud of what I was doing – it was just such a terrible shame that he could never express it to me.

CHAPTER 5
THE COUNTY SET

So here I was in 1985, aged 19 and living in digs in Leicester, a professional county cricketer. My first priority was to try to settle in and feel comfortable with my fellow players.

I would eventually grow to love pre-season, when we would all report back to prepare for the summer ahead – it was a time of hope and expectation, when we all started with a clean slate.

But the start of my very first pre-season with Leicestershire was not an enjoyable experience. I had a run-in with a senior player during my first week. He had a right go at me and I was wasn't happy about it and decided that I didn't want to be there. At the end of that week, I went home to London to see my Mum and of course she wanted to know all about how I was getting on

"I don't want to go back Mum."

"What? Why on earth not? It is all you ever wanted."

"I don't want to go back. In fact, I would rather go and sign on the dole than go back to Leicester."

I had arrived in London on the Friday, and the following day I still had no intention whatsoever of returning to Grace Road. Then I woke up on Sunday morning and thought to myself: "Mum is right. This is what you want to do."

So I got on the train that day, travelled back to Leicester and tried again. I reported back for training the following day, still feeling apprehensive about it all, but this time the atmosphere was completely different. It might have just been all down to me in the first place, but I knuckled down and soon found that I was loving it. I loved running and doing all the exercises and drills.

I shared my meagre accommodation with Lloyd Tennent and Phil Whitticase, who became a good friend, and still is to this day. Money was tight, so we had to share a bedroom. I learnt a lot from Phil, especially in the early days. He was also the man who taught me how to drive.

Before long, my Leicestershire teammates had become like a family to me, a family I wanted to share the good times with, a family that I could share a laugh with.

The first thing I had to learn was not to get ahead of myself – I had to prove that I was going to be good enough to get into the first team, otherwise my dreams would be over before they had even begun.

Incredibly, I spent half of my debut season as twelfth man, making my first appearance against one of the university sides. Nick Cook, the spin bowler, turned round to David Gower and Peter Willey and said: "Look, we should take this lad round with us all year because he bowls well and he bats well, and he can learn more from being with us."

The thing that really clinched it for me was that I had a great fielding arm – I don't want to sound arrogant, but I knew that I was good in the field and that I could save runs, take catches and run people out. It was simply a fact.

I enjoyed being with the players and I was even picked to play in the odd match, and bowled consistently, managing to take 27 wickets in nine matches, including a five-wicket haul.

I remember playing against Gloucester at Cheltenham during the festival week. We arrived at the ground and the rain was coming down in torrents – at one point I looked out of the pavilion and the outfield was flooded. Both sides were convinced that there wouldn't be any play, so when we were invited to join the sponsors in the marquee, it seemed like a good idea.

After we'd all had several drinks, we realised that the rain had gone off. Not only that, but the groundstaff had done a fantastic job of clearing the water from the outfield – we were at a ground with probably the best drainage in the country, which was somewhat unfortunate since by now everybody was extremely merry.

Eventually the umpires decided that we were going to play a 10-overs-a-side match. Oh dear! My outstanding memory of that game was of David Gower trudging out to the wicket, hitting the first ball for four, then playing and missing four times before resorting to playing right-handed. Gower, remember, was regarded by most critics as the best LEFT-HANDED batsman in the world. Somehow, we managed to win the match – I guess because the opposition were even more sozzled than we were.

There was also the added bonus of developing a social life for myself. I had Phil to thank for helping me with that. During my years in London I had never really managed to get out much at night, but I soon got to know one or two good night clubs in Leicester. I would never for one moment suggest that a young athlete should be out on the lash every other night, but you have to let your hair down from time to time.

Don't forget, too, that this was my first time away from home. If I wanted to stay out late, the only person that I had to answer to was myself, just as long as my cricket didn't suffer. And I was never the sort of person to drink vast quantities of alcohol and stay out until the wee small hours anyway. But I did like to have fun, probably because up to that point in my life it had been in pretty short supply.

In particular we used to frequent a place called Caspers. I was enjoying myself and I was enjoying Leicester and its people. Of course, I took a particular interest in the female population of the city, dating quite a few of them during that first year.

My first significant relationship was with a delightful girl called Emma Hobson but the problem for me was that all I was really interested in was my cricket. It was my top priority and it consumed my life. I wanted to give myself a shot at becoming the best player I possibly could and that meant dedicating myself to it.

There are not many teenage girls who would be prepared to play second fiddle to cricket. Remember, too, that I wasn't exactly earning a fortune so I could not afford to wine and dine Emma, or anybody else.

She wanted to settle down, but I was nowhere near ready to do that, although I did care about her. I knew that I had strong feelings for her but eventually she went to Spain to spend some time with her father, and she ended up staying there. Clearly, that marked the end of our relationship.

I was also getting a fair amount of coverage in the local newspaper, *The Leicester Mercury*, which meant that when Phil and I were out about, we were being recognised. Now that presented a whole new set of problems for me, then and at several points in my life.

Anybody who has lived even part of their life in the public eye will tell you that when they are approached by beautiful women there is always a nagging doubt, even if the woman claims to have no idea who you are.

"Is she only interested in me because of who I am?" "Is she with me just because she thinks I might have a few bob?" And, worst of all: "Is she only going out with me because she intends to go and sell her story to the tabloids?"

When you are as insecure as I was, those were all huge issues for me. I wanted to be loved for the person I was, not because some blonde thought she would try and snare a professional cricketer.

There were many other pitfalls. You would be having a quiet meal in a restaurant and people would come up and ask you for your autograph or want to engage you in conversation – now I understand totally that without those people I would not have had the career I did, and I was generally happy to sign autographs, but not when I was eating or when I was obviously involved in an intimate or private conversation with somebody.

At the end of 1985 I decided to go to Australia to continue my development and my cricketing education because I wanted to improve as a player. In those days we only had six-month contracts, which meant that many players signed on the dole during the winter. I didn't want to do that. I managed to secure a contract to play for Port Adelaide thanks to Mike Haysman, an Australian who played for Leicestershire, who recommended me.

I lived above what the Aussies regarded as a hotel, but it was a pub. I stayed with a family called Curtains, in a room above the bar. The good thing about this, of course, was that anytime I fancied a drink I just had to pop downstairs. They made me feel very welcome.

I became friendly with a chap called Craig Bradley, who was also a superb Aussie Rules player, and I quickly realised how fit you had to be to play this game. Craig took me on a few training sessions with him and

I soon realised that I needed to do some serious work on my own fitness – he was at a different level to me.

During my time with Port Adelaide, I made a lot of great friends, people who accepted me and looked after me while I was there. It was a wonderful experience and it did turn me into a better cricketer, which was always the primary goal.

CHAPTER 6
ASHES TO ASHES

So let me pick up the story of the 1986-87 Ashes tour now. We left it with England losing their warm-up games.

I remember thinking: "Surely we have to knuckle down and win some of these games." It got so bad that at one point Martin Johnson famously wrote a piece for *The Independent* in which he expressed the view that we couldn't bat, couldn't bowl and couldn't field. Most of the guys laughed, although it spurred me on.

I realised that Botham, Gower and Lamb were unconcerned and, more important, Gatting and Stewart seemed to be untroubled. I figured that they had done it all before and that they must have known what they were doing. And I need never have doubted it.

Throughout all of this, I was playing well. I was scoring runs, taking wickets and fielding well, and Gatting and Stewart kept encouraging me and telling me to keep at it. I still had no thoughts of making the Test side, however – they were putting me through this so that I could pick up a bit of experience. Whatever they told me to do, I did.

But Botham and Lamb looked as they couldn't have cared less, and I couldn't understand why somebody didn't get a hold of them and give them a good talking to. When it came to practice, Lamby and Gower would both work pretty hard, but Beefy only ever did light network.

And then, as the first Test in Brisbane approached, all three of them really started to get very serious about their practice sessions. We had already been Down Under for a month, but now the proper business was about to get under way, so the fun had to stop.

The day before the match began, the England team was announced – and I was included. I was absolutely overjoyed. Yes, I knew that I had worked hard since we had arrived and I was in decent nick, but being named in the side for the first Test on an Ashes tour was beyond my wildest dreams.

I had been picked on merit and was in the side because I was in good form, but when the reality of it sank in I became really nervous. A huge amount of hype has always accompanied Ashes series, especially at the beginning. The Australians were on home soil and they wanted to beat us, they really wanted to beat us. I guess they were also chuffed to bits that the Poms had included a rookie in their side, somebody they could target with words and deeds.

We had a team dinner on the eve of the Test and Botham, Lamb and Gower made it perfectly clear what was expected of us. "The real stuff starts now. The warm-up games we've played count for nothing. This is what we are here for, to play the Australians and to beat them in their own back yard. It is what we all play cricket for. This is when we turn it on."

As I listened to them, the enormity of what lay ahead hit me between the eyes. I felt the hairs on the back of my neck stand on end, and I felt freezing cold. That night I went to bed and I tossed and turned and didn't sleep a wink. I lay there thinking: "I hope we don't bowl first because I am absolutely knackered and I don't want to let anybody down, especially after everything they have done to make me feel part of it all."

In the end, we won the toss and Mike Gatting decided to bat. Bill Athey batted really well for 76, Gatting made 61, Lamb 40 and Gower 51. And then came Beefy. He was magnificent, scoring 138 with 13 fours and four huge sixes. When I walked out for my first innings for England I was completely numb, wondering how on earth I could ever possibly get bat on ball but when I got to the middle, there to meet me was my hero, Ian Botham. It was a dream come true.

"Just watch the ball Phil, watch the ball," he said.

The first ball I received was from Merv Hughes, who did not have a lot of time for us Poms. It was a bouncer that I managed to get a touch on and I was off the mark, but as I was running towards the non-striker's end I was aware of Hughes doing something. I went over to Botham: "Beefy, I think he just spat at me."

"Don't worry, son, I will sort him out."

The exhibition he put on after that was just astonishing. It was the best hundred I had ever seen, and it didn't matter who was bowling – Botham treated them all with the same disdain. There was one delivery from Greg Matthews, the off-spinner, that he hit straight back at Matthews – the only problem was that the ball was heading for me and as I tried to take evasive action it hit me right in the middle of my back. And it hurt. But I was more concerned about the fact that I had cost him a certain boundary.

Watching him at the other end gave me a bit of confidence and I started playing a few shots and chipped in with 40 before trying to hit one shot too many and getting myself out. But I was there when Botham got his ton and we made 456 all out. It was an experience that I will never forget, and it helped to relax me for the rest of the match.

My first two Test wickets were fairly memorable too – David Boon, caught by Chris Broad, for 10 off a poor delivery and Dean Jones, leg-before for eight. We bowled them out for 248, with Graham Dilley taking five wickets, and then we put them in again. Geoff Marsh made a wonderfully gutsy 110 in the Aussies' second innings but he didn't get a lot of support and they were dismissed for 282. I got Marsh, Greg Ritchie and fast bowler Merv Hughes, and John Emburey chipped in with five wickets. We needed 77 runs to win and knocked them off for the loss of three wickets. In my first Test I had taken five wickets, scored 40 runs and England had got off to a winning start in the Ashes series.

Earlier, I referred to being warned about how the Australian players would sledge us, but the crowd were a lot worse than the players ever were. I would stand out in the field and all I could hear were insults being hurled in my direction. I had been told not to react to it, but when somebody calls you a 'Pommie bastard' for the umpteenth time, it becomes quite a challenge. At one point I could hear some particularly abusive insult being hurled at me and when I turned round I realised it was two youngsters who were responsible for it – but they were being egged on by their parents. I also had various things thrown at me, everything from tennis balls to bananas, and a lot worse besides.

The thing that I had found strangest of all about the cricket was when Botham, at the end of the second day, said: "Right then, let's go and have a beer with them."

I just thought it was odd that after having spent two days batting them out of the game we would then want to go and socialise with them. I was extremely reluctant, but Ian grabbed me by the arm and took me into the Australian dressing room. I sat next to him and looked around at the likes of Allan Border and Greg Ritchie and thought: "What can I say to these guys?" So I just sat there and listened, speaking only when I was spoken to. It was like being in the hotel room with Gower. Once again, I realised that I was very nervous, and you did not want Australian cricketers to know that you were being affected by nerves.

I suppose part of the genius of Botham was that in going into their dressing room he was showing them that he wasn't afraid of them. Not only that, but he won them over as friends and I guess he figured that meant the likes of Mervyn Hughes would not bowl quite as quickly at him. Merv the Swerve, of course, probably tried harder to get Beefy out than any other member of the team.

The thing that struck me was that they talked about everything other than cricket. Here were these guys sharing a laugh together over a cold beer. I thought it was weird. Really weird. We were with them for more than an hour, and when we emerged, the England team bus had already left for the hotel so we had to get a taxi. It was another example of Beefy doing things his own way.

The way it worked was that if the opposition had spent the day in the field, we would go into their dressing room, and vice versa. I was to discover that this was normal practice all over the world, and while Ian subscribed to it, his theory was that by socialising with them he was also getting into their faces and showing them he wasn't afraid of their batsmen or their bowlers.

Some people claim that was a weak Australian side, but let me tell you it was anything but – apart from Marsh, Boon, Hughes and Jones, they also had the incomparable Allan Border as captain and a young batsman called Steve Waugh whom, we were told, was going to be something quite special.

We weren't too bad ourselves. Apart from the batsmen I have already mentioned, we had a bowling attack that consisted of Dilley, Botham and myself, all of whom could generate some pace when required to do so, and the spinners Embury and Phil Edmonds, who hardly gave anything away. We were a handful for any team. We were also an ageing side but I was 20 years old and I used to sit in our dressing room and look round and have to pinch myself because I was playing with a group of legends.

The key to everything was that we all got on well with one another. People talk about the importance of team spirit and I believe that great team spirit comes from winning matches. When you have a group of players together and they beat every side they face it clearly does wonders for their confidence and their sense of camaraderie. Everybody loves winning, but if you are not winning, team spirit tends to be one of the first casualties as players seek to blame teammates.

I was aware of a great spirit within the camp right from day one, even when we were struggling in the warm-up games. Mike Gatting had a very difficult job. How do you captain the likes of Gower, Botham, Lamb, Emburey and Edmonds? The answer is that you don't – you trust them to know what works best for them, and you listen to them when they offer you an opinion.

I realised after the first Test that the management had got it absolutely right when they didn't push the panic button during the warm-up games. By the time we got to Brisbane, everybody was relaxed. But they were also prepared to train hard. People make fun of Mike Gatting's girth, but he was as fit as anybody back then, and he was a very good footballer too.

I know that there is a much more scientific approach to training today, but everybody in our England team was raring to go and able to cope with spending a day in the field in baking temperatures – nobody could do that unless they were in physically good shape. If you take Botham as an example, it would have been impossible to get through the number of overs in a day that he did unless he was fit. Remember, too, that he played a bit of professional football. He liked people to believe that he knocked back the beer and didn't do any training, but he worked as hard as everybody else. He had to, because he was a naturally big man and had to take care of himself.

There was another big difference between then and now. England went out to Australia for the 2010-11 Ashes series with a group of players on central contracts, accompanied by batting coaches, bowling coaches, wicket keeping coaches, nutritionists, psychologists, physical trainers, psychologists – they even had their own chef. We had a manager, Peter Lush, a coach, Mickey Stewart, a physio, Laurie Brown and a group of 16 players.

I was stick thin, and weighed just over 10 stone, so the first thing that Mickey, Laurie and Gatts said to me was that I could eat whatever I wanted because they wanted me to put on weight.

Laurie was an amazing man. He was not only our physio but he also acted as the team doctor. Mickey organised all the practice sessions, tactics and suchlike and Peter Lush did everything else.

So we had made the perfect start to the series.

The second Test started on 28 November and took place in Perth on a perfect batting wicket. We batted first and Chris Broad scored 192, Bill Athey 96, David Gower 136 and Jack Richards 133. I only managed to make 11 runs but in a total of 592 for eight declared it hardly mattered. Graham Dilley grabbed four wickets but bowling was hard work and we did well to bowl them out for 401. My sole wicket was that of fast bowler

Geoff Lawson but my abiding memory of that match was that it was sheer hard work for all the bowlers. I suddenly realised that perhaps Test cricket was not as easy as I had thought.

We made 199 for eight declared in our second innings, set the Australians an unlikely victory target of 391, and when Dilley got Boon out for a duck with just one run on the board we briefly dared to dream about bowling them out, but in the end they survived comfortably enough, scoring 197 for four. I went wicketless. The match finished in a draw, but we had by far the better of it.

And so we moved to Adelaide, where the third Test began on 12 December. Because of the time I had spent there the previous year, I was really looking forward to the match as I knew that a lot of the friends I had made were going to come along to watch. It is a great city and, for me, the ground is second only to Lord's. I was very excited about it all.

It turned out to be another pretty flat wicket, ideal for batting, and this time it was the turn of the Aussies to dominate with the bat in the first innings. They scored 514 for five declared with David Boon hitting a century, Dean Jones 93, Border 70, Greg Matthews 73, and Steve Waugh 79. My 32 overs cost 128 runs for the wicket of Greg Ritchie. It was tough, really tough. We made 455 thanks to centuries from Chris Broad and Gatting. I finished four not out.

There was never going to be a result, but Australia went through the motions and scored 201 for three declared. We had been set a nominal target of 261 but had little or no time in which to score the runs. So the match finished in another draw.

Just before the Boxing Day Test in Melbourne, all the players' wives and girlfriends came out to join them. You have to remember that they had been apart from their loved ones for the thick end of three months.

Yes, you could argue that they were in a privileged position, representing their country in the most famous series of them all, but in those days there were no contracts and the money was pretty poor. Botham would have been the only one who was making a really comfortable living from the game.

One of the traditions is that on Christmas Day all the players have to wear fancy dress for dinner. We each received a letter and inside the envelope was a piece of paper with an initial written on it. We had to come as a character that began with that letter – inside my envelope was the letter 'D' and I headed off to the fancy dress shop with Gladstone Small and his girlfriend, Lois (they later got married), wondering what on earth I could wear. I couldn't find anything and eventually the proprietor approached me with a glittering red dress.

"What about this?" he said.

"What about it? What has that got to do with the letter 'D'?"

"Diana Ross. You will be perfect."

"No way am I going dressed as Diana Ross."

At that point Lois said that she agreed with the guy, that I would make a great Diana Ross, so in the end I agreed and we left the shop with the red dress and a black wig. On Christmas Day I went into Gladstone's room and Lois applied the make-up. I managed to find a pair of size ten high-heeled shoes which were agony to walk in – how do women do that? She looked me up and down and said: "Phil, why don't you get rid of your moustache, then you will be perfect."

Just about everybody had a moustache back then, and I was no exception. I guess that I thought it made me look older. I had agreed to wear a red dress, black wig, women's shoes and make-up, but I drew the line at shaving off my moustache. And so I walked into the dining room and everybody fell about, and the thing is that almost everybody told me that if I removed my 'tache I would be an absolute ringer for Diana Ross. I was mortified, but it was a real fun day and everybody had a great time.

Another tradition was that the English press, who spent the tour with us, put on a play in which they made fun of the players – there was nothing malicious in it, and everybody had a laugh. We used to have a drink with the journalists and socialise with them and regarded them as part of the touring party – I cannot imagine that happening now.

Before the day was over we also did a live broadcast back to the UK with Noel Edmonds, who was as much a part of Christmas back then as turkey and stuffing.

By now, Botham's family were with him and he had announced that he wanted his own room and, obviously, his request was granted. When your family fly halfway across the world to be with you, the last thing you are going to want to do is share a room with a spotty teammate.

And so to the fourth Test, more commonly known as the Boxing Day Test. It was played at the Melbourne Cricket Ground, which is one of the best venues on the planet. Before play got under way, we were out on the field loosening up and as I looked round I became aware of Australian fans holding up newspaper pictures of me dressed as Diana Ross. "We love you Daffy, we love you," they were shouting. They were also holding up signs poking fun at Beefy and Gatts, but this was a good thing because it told us that they respected us.

Gradually the ground filled up and when we came out to bowl the place was packed and it made the hairs on the back of my neck stand on end. We all knew how significant this match was – win it and we would take the series.

Graham Dilley was injured, so I opened the bowling with Gladstone

Small, who bowled really well and ended up taking five wickets.

I thought that my opening spell in Melbourne was one of my best ever for England but it was one of those days where I had no luck at all. Beefy had been a serious doubt for the match because of a side strain but obviously we really wanted him to play so he had a couple of injections and announced that he would be able to bowl but not at full pace, or anything close to it. I reckon he was about 70% fit, but it didn't prevent him from mopping up the other five wickets as we bowled them out for 141 in just 54.4 overs. I bowled 11 overs for 30 runs. Apart from Dean Jones, who made 59, no Australian batsman made it to 20.

After watching Botham get his wickets I went up to Gatting and said: "What's going on here? I've just bowled a superb spell and got nothing for it, and Beefy, who isn't fit, gets five."

"You just have to accept it, that's the magic of the man," came the reply. And he was right. The thing with Botham was that he got wickets with dreadful deliveries and I joked with Gatting that perhaps I should deliberately start bowling badly, just to see what would happen.

Chris Broad made another century and Gatting and Lamb chipped in with 40 and 43 respectively as we made 349 to give us a first innings lead of 208. I made seven before edging a Craig McDermott delivery that was caught by Greg Matthews.

We had utterly dominated Australia for two days and could taste a series victory, and when they came in to bat for a second time it turned out to be a real team effort from the England bowling attack. I claimed the wicket of Dean Jones, Gladstone took another couple of wickets, as did John Emburey, and Phil Edmonds claimed three. There was also a run-out as the Australians subsided to 194. We had won by an innings and 14 runs inside three days but, better than that, we had also won the series, leading 2-0 with just one Test remaining.

It was about that time that I finally understood that we were playing for a tiny trophy that wouldn't normally attract a second glance, a little urn purported to contain the burnt remains of a cricket bail after the 'obituary' of English cricket appeared in *The Sporting Times* in 1882 after Australia beat England at The Oval. For all that I had followed cricket, I hadn't a clue we were playing for this terracotta urn, and that the original was locked away at Lord's. And the full significance didn't register with me until I got back to England and people kept asking: "Do you realise what you've done?"

One of my abiding memories of that Melbourne match, and indeed of the tour, was of the huge numbers of English people who suddenly seemed to appear to cheer us on. From that point of view, there is nothing better than being a member of a successful England sporting team, whether it is cricket, football or tiddlywinks. The English support was just amazing and everywhere we went, they were there too, patting us on the backs, telling us how proud they were to be English. It brought a lump to my throat on more than one occasion.

CHAPTER 7
I'M STILL STANDING

For a rookie like me it seemed too good to be true. What an incredible way to start my Test career, beating the Aussies on their home patch – and beating them really well. We got back to the dressing room and the champagne was flowing and enjoying it all with us was Elton John. No, that is not a misprint – the one and only Elton John, probably the greatest pop star of his generation, helped us to celebrate. For me, it was utterly surreal. First of all I'd had to get used to playing with, and sharing rooms with, my heroes and now I was sharing champagne with a music legend.

To be truthful, what we had achieved on the cricket field didn't really sink in. Sure, everybody was celebrating and knocking back the booze but I didn't quite understand what it meant. Bill Athey, who sports a British bulldog tattoo and is English through and through, was really going for it. The atmosphere was superb and we had a great party but it took some time before the enormity of it dawned on me.

Elton John is a man who has had some bad press throughout his career. He admitted taking drugs and then owned up to being an alcoholic, and the documentary *Tantrums and Tiaras* probably didn't do him any good at all, but I found him a warm, genuine man. It was a pleasure to be in his company, and he was always genuinely interested in what I had to say.

He had been putting on some concerts in Australia but basically because of Lamb, Botham and Gower, all of whom he knew, he ended up following us for most of the tour. He was like a lucky mascot, but what a mascot to have!

It had all started when we went to see him in concert in Sydney and we were invited backstage to meet him. He became like a member of the family in the end. It seemed that every time we won a match, Elton threw a party for us, and no expense was spared. As you can imagine, where Elton went, so did the stars – on one occasion I had to do a double take as I was sure that I had seen George Michael. Of course it was George Michael.

I asked Elton for an introduction and could hardly speak for nerves, even though this guy wasn't much older than I was. I don't suppose that I realised the enormity of it all, but I can tell you that I was having such great fun, on and off the pitch. All of this was beyond my wildest dreams. We made sure that we celebrated and enjoyed our victories, but we were always ready for the next challenge.

And so, with hardly any time to recover, we were off to Perth, where I made my one-day debut for England at the Waca on 1 January in the first match of the Benson and Hedges Challenge, which also involved Pakistan and the West Indies. By this time, we had our foot on their throats and we were determined that we were not going to ease off. Broad, Lamb and Botham all hit half centuries as we made 272 for six, and then I grabbed three wickets as we dismissed them for 235 to record yet another victory. Cricket against Australia wasn't meant to be this easy, and we would discover in the years to come that it would never be that way again. We had hurt their pride and in Allan Border they had a captain who vowed that it would never happen again – but that was for the future.

Next up were the West Indies, whom we beat largely due to a terrific bowling performance by Graham Dilley, who took four wickets. And then it was the turn of Pakistan, and this time we had Chris Broad to thank – again! He rattled off 97 and we won by three wickets to reach the final, where we once again had to face Pakistan at the Waca. We bowled them out for 166 and although I didn't take any wickets, I was happy enough with my performance. Not surprisingly, we reached our target with almost 10 overs to spare.

This was a formidable Pakistan team – it included Imran Khan, Javed Miandad and Wasim Akram – and the West Indies side we defeated featured Gordon Greenidge, Desmond Haynes, Viv Richards, Joel Garner, Michael Holding and a young Courtney Walsh. We were absolutely flying – in six days in Perth we had played four one-days against three of the best teams on the planet and we had won the lot.

And then, on 10 January, it was back to Test cricket, with the fifth and final Test beginning in Sydney. Quite a few of the players still had their wives out with them so we stayed in apartments near Bondi Beach. There were a number of single fellows who were on their own, including me, and each couple was asked to look after one of the singles and I ended up with Botham, who had his own apartment with his family. I am sure they didn't want me around, but that was what Mickey Stewart and Mike Gatting wanted.

We also had a team room, which was where Peter Lush had his wife and daughter staying. They made us welcome but it reached the point where the players felt they couldn't go in there to have a drink because they would be intruding upon Peter and his family. In the end, we decided to use Beefy's as the team room and whenever we would go in, Elton would already be there and we would sit and chat. At the beginning, most of us had been overawed by this man, but now he had become just like one of the lads.

I would talk to him about my cricket and how much I was enjoying the tour. We just had normal everyday conversations, the type of thing two friends would chat about. And we would also enjoy a laugh and a joke. He was no longer Elton John, superstar; instead, he was Elton John, friend and cricket fan.

Maybe he recognised that although I tried to put on a front, I was somewhat in awe of my teammates because he seemed to go out of his way to look after me and check that I was getting on all right. I treat people as I find them, and he was like a father to me during that time in Australia, a kind and caring man with only my best interests at heart.

It was to be the start of a long relationship. For my benefit year in 2004, he sent me one of his tour jackets to auction.

There was another man who looked after me during that tour. Through Ian Botham, I got to know David English, who followed us for most of the tour and went out of his to make sure that I was all right, spend time in my company and take me out for a bite to eat. He even described himself as my Dad, and to this day, he still does.

After everything that had gone before, the Sydney Test was the only real low point for me. Dilley was fit again and because Gladstone had bowled so well in the Melbourne Test, I was the one who missed out. At least Gatts and Stewart had the decency to take me to one side and say: "Listen, we are leaving you out for this one Phil. Gladstone bowled well in the last Test and Dilley is back fit and has also been bowling well and is coming back in so we have to leave somebody out. And we can't play four seamers because the wicket will turn and we need to have both spinners in the team. A seamer has to go."

Perhaps I made it too easy for them. "I totally understand that Gladstone took five wickets, so that's fair enough."

By this point some of the players felt the job had already been done and were starting to think about home, but I was desperate to keep playing.

I was angry that I had been left out, but I accepted that the selectors knew best, and it was only years later when I looked back on it that I realised how unfairly I had been treated. They were wrong to drop me. At my age they should have kept playing me. I didn't know it then, but it would be the first of 14 times that I would be dropped by England.

Australia won the toss and scored 345 runs, but that only tells part of the story. Dean Jones contributed 184 of those runs and the next best was Border, who made 34. Gladstone was on fire, and took five wickets. Before we knew where we were, the Aussies had us reeling at 17 for three but Gower and Jack Richards got the ship back on course before John Emburey came in and scored a really gutsy 69. We were dismissed for 275 runs and trailed our hosts by 70 runs.

Emburey then performed heroics with the ball, taking seven second-innings wickets as we bowled out Australia for 251. Steve Waugh showed us the sign of things to come when he came in at 115 for five and dug in to make 73 invaluable runs.

Our victory target was 322. Broad made 17, Athey 31, Gower 37, Lamb 3 and when Botham was dismissed first ball we were 102 for five and the match appeared to be all over bar the shouting. But Mike Gatting had other ideas and played a tremendous captain's innings. When he was out for 96, he had put on 121 with Jack Richards and we were 233 for six.

Unfortunately, we had all but run out of batsmen by that stage and when Embers was unable to repeat his first-innings heroics it really was a case of game over. They dismissed us for 264 and won by 55 runs to salvage some pride from a series in which we had dominated them in most departments. Chris Broad was voted man of the series – he scored 487 runs and averaged 69.57. For my part, I scored 77 runs and averaged 19.25 with the bat and took wickets at 49.55.

Our tour still wasn't over, however, as we now had to play Australia and West Indies in a triangular tournament, the Benson and Hedges World Series Cup. We suffered a couple of heavy defeats at the hands of Australia but did well enough against the West Indies to make sure that we reached the best-of-three final, where we faced the hosts again. I had bowled decently enough but because I was coming in well down the order I never really had the opportunity to show what I could do with the bat.

Some strange things happen when you play cricket around the world. During one of the one-day internationals at Melbourne. I was about to open the bowling and became aware that golf balls were landing on the outfield. I pulled up and looked to the top of the ground and there was a man with a golf club, hitting balls at me.

The first final took place at the Melbourne Cricket Ground on 8 February and we restricted them to 171 for eight. I took two wickets and Dilley claimed three. Botham opened our innings alongside Chris Broad and although Broad was dismissed cheaply, quickly followed by Bill Athey, Beefy scored 71 off 52 balls and Gower struck 45 off 47 deliveries and we duly strolled to victory.

Then it was off to Sydney for the second final on 11 February – we had played our first tour match against Queensland Country on 18 October.

It was a day-night match, which was a rarity in those days, and batting was not easy. Broad top-scored for us with 53, I made one and we limped to 187 for nine. It was surely not going to be good enough. Incredibly, it was. The Australians couldn't get into their stride although we also bowled really well – Beefy took three wickets for 26 runs and I bagged a couple for 34. They could only reach 179, and we had won another trophy.

Because I had done pretty well in the one-day matches, I suddenly became aware that I was being branded a one-day specialist but I loved Test cricket, performed the role I was given to the best of my ability and did what I was told to do.

Finally, we could go home though and I could set about proving that I had what it took to compete in the five-day game. I should say that I didn't want to go home. As far as I was concerned, the guys I had spent the winter with were my new family and I wanted to carry on playing cricket with them. It felt like a family because people cared about me, cared about what I was thinking and about what I had to contribute, and that was a big deal for me.

We got home to England in February – it was hardly the most appetising prospect, and I was gutted. I loved that tour so much, apart from Sydney, that I wanted it to go on forever. I felt that it was an environment in which I couldn't be hurt because there was so much protection around me, and there were so many individuals looking out for me.

I felt loved and I felt wanted. Never for one moment had I felt homesick. Given the chance to have remained in Australia for a further 12 months with the same group of guys, I would have jumped at the opportunity.

When we got back, there was a good deal of positive media, but there was no question of open-top bus tours or MBEs and/or OBEs for the players. Not that any of us cared a jot about that because we all knew only too well that we had achieved something special. Yes, there are times when I look at the way the England side is feted today and I ask myself: "Why didn't we get that?" It would have been brilliant to have come home and been acclaimed by the fans, but it wasn't to be – they were different times.

Besides, how could we possibly know how long it would be before another England team would repeat the feat? I take my hat off to the side that went to Australia in 2010-11 because it was the first time in all these years that our cricketers had gone into an Ashes series Down Under as favourites. They were under tremendous pressure to deliver, and did precisely that. You can say whatever you want about the relative strength of the Australian team, but they will always give their all to avoid defeat.

The player who made the biggest impression on me was Allan Border, whom I had already played against in county cricket when he represented Essex. During a county match at Southend I took 13 wickets and got Border out twice and before the Ashes series began, he was quoted in a newspaper article as saying that he was going to go after me, so there was a bit of needle between us.

As a cricketer he was such a tough player, somebody who hated to give his wicket away. I always remember how tough and aggressive he was. You always felt with him that he wanted to fight you all the time. He was a brilliant batsman, clearly had the potential to become a very good captain, and losing was anathema to him.

The other Australian who left a mark on me was Steve Waugh, who was
at the start of his career. He scored a few runs but didn't have a brilliant
series but the Australians had identified him as a great player for the
future and they had made up their minds to stick with him, come what
may. Eventually, of course, he came good and it obviously benefited him
to be captained by Border. As things worked out, that Ashes series was to
be a turning point for Australian cricket, but nobody knew it at the time.

They identified a number of good young players and decided to give
them a chance to develop into Test cricketers, and thus the likes of
Border, Steve and Mark Waugh, Mark Taylor, Ian Healy and, later,
Shane Warne and Glenn McGrath began to emerge and turned into
world beaters.

In my case, I thought, naively, that every tour would be as good as the
1986-87 one had been, but I was to learn that wasn't the case at all.

On 18 February 1987, I turned 21 and I longed to still be in Australia
celebrating it with my teammates, but it was not to be. Instead, I
celebrated it in a nightclub called Harveys, in Leicester, with Phil
Whitticase and a couple of my Leicestershire teammates.

Soon afterwards, I went to Dominica with Faron, one of my brothers –
I had earned a decent amount playing for England so told him that I
would pay for him, so we flew out there, booked into our hotel but then
decided that we needed a car to get around. My brother couldn't drive,
but I had this provisional licence that I had applied for when I had been
in Australia as a teenager.

I duly produced the licence and was told that I could actually take my
driving test in Dominica. "So if I pass my test, will I be able to drive
straight away?" I asked.

"Yes you can," came the reply. It was a no-brainer. I duly took my test and, lo and behold, I passed so I was able to hire a car for the duration of the stay. However, this was only a licence that allowed me to drive in Dominica, so I am not sure how much use it actually was. When I returned to England I still had to sit a proper driving test.

We had only been in Dominica for a short while and I turned to my brother and said: "This doesn't feel right. I want to be home."

"But this is your real home Phil."

"It may be the place where I was born, but it is not home. England is home. I don't want to be here. I want to go back to Leicester."

I had spent the first nine years of my life in this place but now I felt like a stranger; what's more, I couldn't actually understand the locals. They were speaking in a kind of broken French that I had grown up with, but it meant nothing to me; they might as well have been talking double-Dutch. Even now, my brothers will talk about Dominica and ask me if I remember this or that, and I am never able to do so.

I took my own family and my in-laws to Dominica in 2008 and that was totally different. I enjoyed the place and loved being there with them. Only then did I realise what a spectacularly beautiful place it was and how lucky I had been to spend the early part of my childhood there.

But in 1987 all that I was interested in was getting out of there and returning to Leicester, to my comfort zone. People regarded me then and now as being a confident, outgoing person, but nothing could be further from the truth. I am actually shy and reserved, and consider that I have always been able to put on a good act for people. I am not comfortable with strangers and I don't like being in places that I don't know.

Being a successful sportsman means subjecting yourself to the media. I knew and understood that it was part and parcel of the job and that I would to be interviewed by journalists, especially when I was on England duty, or in the build-up to a Test series, or after a really good display with bat or ball. Most of my colleagues loved it, but I didn't.

The truth is that I was scared of the media, and I guess that I was frightened that eventually one day I would sit in front of a journalist who would be able to see right through me, and realise that I wasn't this confident, outgoing individual that I tried to be, that it was all an act. Back in those days, journalists were a very different animal – it seems to me that if you are successful today, they want to find a way to knock you down, but back in the early days of my career I honestly believe that most of them just wanted to see the best in me. Maybe they really did hope that I would turn out to be 'the next Botham'. But that didn't stop the terror.

Another huge difference, of course, is that today's sportsmen are coached in how to deal with and speak to the media; they know what to say and, more importantly, they know what not to say. My generation had none of that, so you always had to go with your instinct and hope that you got it right, that you said the correct thing.

Inevitably, of course, journalists would write critical articles and when that happened I wouldn't come out of my house for days. I suppose that I felt a degree of shame and embarrassment, and it was extremely difficult for me to deal with. That had nothing to do with a lack of coaching in media relations – it was all about the person I was. I wish it could have been different, but my feeling was that if a journalist saw fault with me then I was convinced that everybody else saw and felt the same thing.

I was a young cricketer who had broken into the England side at a very young age, I had played in a successful Ashes team in Australia, and I was playing for Leicestershire, a great county – I should have been on Cloud Nine, with not a care in the world. Instead, I sometimes found myself feeling worthless, and all because of some of the stuff I had gone through at home and at school.

CHAPTER 8
IS THIS YOUR CAR, SIR?

After I returned from the Ashes tour, lots of things changed for me. The most obvious was that I was given a sponsored BMW 3-series to drive. It was a beautiful car.

I never drink and drive, and get very angry with people who do. I was out one night with Phil Whitticase and a couple of the other guys and I said that I would take my car if somebody else was prepared to drive it.

Chris Munden offered to drive back, so I parked the car and off we went to Caspers and had a few drinks. To put none too fine a point on it, I was hammered at the end of the night. I couldn't have driven if I had wanted to, and I certainly didn't want to so David said: "Okay then, so I am driving."

I handed him the keys and climbed into the passenger seat of the car, which had my name emblazoned on the side. We all lived in digs near Blaby, so David was driving along the Welford Road, and we passed Leicester Tigers ground, just as a police car overtook us and decided to pull us over.

The policeman got out, peered into the car and said: "Ah DeFreitas, pissed again I see. Have you been driving this car?"

"No, no officer, of course not. My mate is driving, and he has not had

75

a drink all night."

"Okay then off you go, but be careful."

Five minutes later we were pulled up again. The officer once again looked into the car and said: "DeFreitas, I see you are pissed again." I found this a bit disconcerting because I didn't get drunk that often, and he had said almost exactly the same as the first officer. It was as if some message was being sent around the Leicestershire police force.

"Have you just swapped seats?"

"No, I haven't. My mate's driving."

"Okay, off you go. Just be careful."

That was the start of it. From that point on, whenever we used to go out for a drink, if I got tipsy it seemed that everybody not only knew, but they also knew where we had been.

In those early days, we used to go to Caspers on Wednesday, Harvey's on Thursday and another club called Joker's on a Friday or Saturday.

There was another occasion when Phil and I went out in the middle of a game. We each had a pint and then went on to soft drinks and as we walked around the club we bumped straight into the two daughters of Mike Turner, the Leicestershire chief executive. We were wetting ourselves and begged the girls not to say that they had seen us because we knew that we would be in big trouble, even though we were drinking water.

They assured us our secret was safe and off home we went. I was in bed by midnight, but when I got up the next morning and headed to Grace Road I was still in a panic. I walked up the stairs into the ground, with Turner's office on the left and as I drew level with it, the door flew open and he said: "In my office now."

He demanded to know what we had been up to the previous evening.

But Phil and I could never be sure whether it was his daughters who had told him or whether it was the police because he had a good relationship with one of the inspectors, who would always let him know when we had been seen out and about. The BMW was a great car but it was too conspicuous and landed me in some spots.

I could do nothing without everybody knowing about it. But I was single and I was just doing the stuff that young single men do. I had fun, I went out with girls and I had a drink. It was hardly the crime of the century.

And it didn't affect my performance on the field. In 1986, which was my first full season for the county, I took 94 wickets, including a best of seven for 44, and I took seven five-wicket hauls. My 27 matches that year also included 645 runs, featured my first century and a couple of fifties. I also seemed to reserve my best performances for matches when we were really struggling, hitting a century against Kent at Canterbury after we had been reduced to 40 for six.

If I had ever felt that I didn't belong, I now knew that I deserved my place in the side. My only regret was that I did not quite manage to reach 100 wickets. But there would be plenty of chances to put that right, or so I thought. In the end, I never again surpassed 80 wickets, and 44 for seven would be my career-best figures for Leicestershire. There would, however, be plenty more match-winning performances to come, with both bat and ball.

CHAPTER 9
YOU'RE OUT SON

In 1987 we had a home series against Pakistan, and having played against Wasim Akram, Javed Miandad and Imran Khan during the one-day matches in Australia, I couldn't wait to face them again on English wickets.

Before the Tests, we faced them in three one-day internationals. The first two were shared, and I bowled pretty well in both. Then it came down to the decider at Edgbaston. Again, I bowled well without taking any wickets and we restricted them to 213. When it was our turn to bat, wickets fell quickly and only Mike Gatting, who made 40, really got going and suddenly I found myself out in the middle with England in all sorts of trouble. I swung the bat and scored 33 off 22 balls, hitting four fours and a six as we won with three balls to spare.

I was chosen for the first Test, a rain-affected draw at Old Trafford. Neil Fairbrother made his debut, in front of his home fans, and he was really nervous before he went out to bat. I told him to relax and enjoy himself. Tim Robinson scored a bucket-load of runs, and there really isn't a lot else to say about the game – we lost far too much play to the weather to ever get a result. I was chomping at the bit to get going in the second Test, which was played at Lord's – I'd bowled for my country in

Australia, but there was nothing like doing it at HQ.

We'd done well in Australia and had established a tremendous team spirit, but then the county season got underway and one or two players were out of touch, while a couple of others who hadn't been in the side, or even been considered, were suddenly called up. To me, it seemed a pretty odd way to treat people. If you have a winning team, surely you stick with it and move forward with it, perhaps making the odd tweak? But no!

Whether you were a batsman or a bowler, you were expected to be at your very best at all times, and I am sorry, but that is impossible, no matter how good you are. And it is the biggest difference between now and then – you were maybe allowed one or two failures back then before being dropped, whereas England stick with players today and give them the chance to get a feel for Test cricket.

People talk about success being down to mental strength but, in my opinion, that is complete rubbish. Maybe they have had a bit of luck with a bad ball that has taken a wicket or with a dropped catch, and they have gone on to take a few wickets or score a ton. It is about taking advantage of the good breaks when they come along.

I put on a front, trying to give people the impression that I was a really confident individual and that nothing got me down, but as you now know, nothing could have been further from the truth, so you can imagine how I felt when I was dropped for the second Test against Pakistan in 1987. At first I thought somebody must have made a mistake. Why on earth would they drop me after a drawn Test? It made no sense whatsoever, and I felt devastated, especially as nobody bothered to pick up a phone and tell me why I had been dropped.

Throughout my 10 years as an England player, nobody ever made the effort to get to know me or find out what made me tick – if they had done, they might have handled dropping me as often as they did slightly differently. Sometimes I reacted pretty negatively to some of the things that were said to me within the England set-up, but it wasn't because I didn't want to be there or because I didn't agree with the way the side was run – it was simply my way of dealing with what I saw as the poor way I was treated. Maybe if I had been a stronger character or a more outgoing individual I might have sat down with the captain or chairman of selectors and asked them to explain why I was dropped and to tell me what I needed to do to get back in and nail down my spot.

The Lord's Test ended in a draw as well, and so off they went to Headingley and I was left out again as Pakistan thrashed us by an innings and 18 runs, despite the fact that Neil Foster took eight wickets in Pakistan's only innings. The real damage was done by Imran Khan, who took 10 wickets in the match, and Wasim Akram, who took five. They swung the ball all over the place and were well-nigh unplayable. That didn't make me feel any better though. I still couldn't understand why I had been left out.

The fourth Test took place at Edgbaston – England had to win it and the final match at The Oval to take the series, but they still couldn't find room for me in the team. It was another draw. And I wasn't recalled for the final Test either, where Pakistan scored an unbelievable 708 runs. Abdul Qadir then mesmerised the England batsmen with his spin bowling, taking seven wickets as the hosts were bowled out for 232. Fortunately, Gatting played a captain's innings second time around and saved the match thanks to a wonderful 150, but we lost the series 1-0 and I was pretty miserable.

CHAPTER 10
ONE DAY AT A TIME

Apart from my Test career, I played 103 one-day internationals for my country and have some outstanding memories.

For starters, there was the 1987 World Cup, which was held in India and Pakistan and lasted for a month, starting in October. Perhaps the organisers of the current competition should take note – it lost nothing for 'only' lasting a month. Eight teams took part, split into two groups and we played the other teams in our groups twice each – it meant that freak results would not affect the overall outcome and that the teams that would progress would be the ones who had performed most consistently. The top two teams in each group would meet in the semi-finals, with the final being played in Calcutta on 8 November.

Group A consisted of India, Australia, New Zealand and Zimbabwe, the only non-Test playing nation in the competition at that time, and Group B featured ourselves, Pakistan, Sri Lanka and West Indies.

One of the highlights of the tournament came for me in the foyer of the Lahore Hilton when I bumped straight into one of all-time heroes, the one and only Muhammad Ali, probably the greatest heavyweight boxer who ever lived, and certainly the most charismatic.

Ali was a guest in Pakistan on the back of his status as a Muslim and as a living sporting legend. I had just completed a net session in the steaming humidity of the Gaddafi Stadium and entered the hotel with sweat streaming from my body. I know that Ali was not a cricket fan, so he definitely had no idea who I was. Perhaps he mistook me for a boxer. He did the Ali shuffle and the pair of us shadow-boxed for a few moments, much to the bemusement of his local hosts.

Next up for us was a group game against West Indies at Guiranwala. With sunset around 5pm, matches started at 9.30am. Our hotel in Lahore was several hours away by road from Guiranwala, so we had to leave the hotel at 4.40am without having time for breakfast. That didn't stop Mike Gatting, tucking into several cans of cold baked beans on the way to the venue.

As inspired as I had been by meeting Ali, instead of uprooting stumps against West Indies, I found myself throwing up halfway through my run-up, but we did go on to win. So how did I come to throw up? The day before the match, our physio had told us to take lots of fluids on board to stop us from becoming dehydrated. I drank gallons and gallons of water, but grew fed up with it so decided to polish off three or four cans of Fanta. It was not one of my better ideas. Coming in during my seventh or eighth over of the day, I knew that I was in trouble and stopped halfway through my run-up and did what had to be done on the outfield. To make matters worse, I dropped the ball into the sick. They brought some sawdust out to get rid of the mess I had made but I couldn't help smiling during the next over when I saw Gladstone Small polishing the ball.

In the next game, I managed to do the impossible when I dismissed Javed Miandad leg before wicket, allegedly the first time the Pakistan batsman had fallen in such a way on home soil. Neutral umpires probably helped break that particular duck.

On 17 October we thrashed Sri Lanka by 108 runs in Peshawar but a couple of days later we were up against Pakistan again and they beat us once more, by seven wickets. Fortunately, comfortable victories over Sri Lanka and West Indies saw us through to the semi-finals, where we faced India.

In the other semi, Pakistan took on Australia. Naturally, the fans and the organisers wanted a Pakistan-India final in front of 90,000 people at Eden Gardens in Calcutta. But Australia and ourselves had other plans. The Aussies scored 267 for six in Lahore, thanks to impressive batting by David Boon and Dean Jones. They then took three early Pakistan wickets and despite the efforts of Javed Miandad and Imran Khan, bowled them out for 252 to reach the final.

Meanwhile in Mumbai (or Bombay as it was then), India won the toss and put us in to bat. It was a strange feeling, knowing that almost every person in the ground wanted us to lose. And it seemed things were going India's way when we stumbled to 79 for two, but then Graham Gooch scored a quite magnificent 115 and was given able support by Mike Gatting, who made 56, and we reached 254 for six. The day before the match, Goochie had been preparing to face the Indian spinners by hitting sweep shot after sweep shot. Never was a batsman better prepared for what was to come than he was. It was brilliant to watch a man at the very top of his game like that.

According to the script Sunil Gavaskar would hit the winning runs and then go on to hit a match-winning century in the final, in what was to be his final international match. Instead, I bowled him as they lost three wickets for 73, and I was not a popular man. Despite the efforts of Mohammed Azharuddin, who top-scored with 64 off 74 balls, they were always struggling and we dismissed them for 219.

The final would be between England and Australia at Eden Gardens on 8 November. The atmosphere was electric. We were told there were 90,000 in the ground but I am certain it was more, and there were fireworks going off all over the place. I had never experienced anything like it. Walking out to the middle in those circumstances was incredibly intimidating – the hairs on the back of my neck were standing on end and I realised that this was why I played cricket. This was what it was all about.

Australia won the toss and elected to bat. Gladstone Small and I opened the bowling and we didn't bowl particularly well. Boon carried on where he had left off in the semi-final, hitting 75, and Mike Veletta smashed 45 runs from 31 deliveries as the Aussies scored 65 runs from the last six overs to score 253 for five. Eddie Hemmings got two of the wickets and Graham Gooch bowled Craig McDermott. It was a target that was easily within reach, but we were on the back foot from the start when Tim Robinson was bowled for a duck with the first delivery.

We recovered, with Bill Athey and Mike Gatting going along nicely, and then Gatts attempted a sweep and was gone for 41. Lamb came in and made a quickfire 45, but the run-rate was rising all the time. I was out for 17 after hitting two fours and six in 10 deliveries. I had a chance to win it for us with the bat and was so frustrated that I hadn't been able to pull it off. We needed 17 from the last over, but couldn't get them and eventually reached 246 for eight.

That was a bitter disappointment, and one of the regrets of my career is that I did not play on a winning World Cup team. To have achieved it in India, in front of huge, cricket-mad crowds would have been something extra special, but it wasn't to be.

The 1992 World Cup was held in Australia and New Zealand during February and March. It was the first to feature coloured clothing, white balls and black sightscreens as matches were played under floodlights. We went into the tournament with a really strong team – Ian Botham opened with Graham Gooch and we had lots of good all-rounders, including Dermot Reeve, Chris Lewis, Derek Pringle and myself. We also had Allan Lamb and Graeme Hick. We really fancied our chances of going one better this time.

There were eight teams taking part, including South Africa, who had just been readmitted to international cricket, and the tournament was played in a round robin format, featuring 36 matches, plus two semi-finals and a final.

In the end, ourselves, New Zealand, Pakistan and South Africa qualified for the semi-finals. Pakistan was extremely fortunate to get through to the last four. We played them in a group match in Adelaide and dismissed them for 74 and were cruising towards victory when the game was washed out, giving Pakistan the point they needed to pip Australia.

We played South Africa in the semi-final and the match ended in farcical circumstances. There was a rain delay and the rules in force at the time revised South Africa's target from 22 runs from 13 balls to 21 runs from one delivery. We were delighted to be in another final, but nobody was particularly happy about the way it was achieved.

Pakistan, meanwhile, brushed New Zealand aside, so we faced them in the final at Melbourne's MCG.

Pringle took two early wickets before Imran Khan and Javed Miandad came together to add 139 for the third wicket. The only blessing for us was that the run rate wasn't exactly what you would call spectacularly quick. And we dropped Imran when he had scored just nine runs in 16 overs. Inzamam-ul-Haq and Wasim Akram threw bat at ball in the late stage of the Pakistan innings and saw them to 249 for six. It was a competitive total, but one which we should have reached with some comfort.

Nothing is ever that straightforward though. Graeme Hick went cheaply, but Neil Fairbrother and Allan Lamb saw us on to 141 for four. And then Wasim entered the fray and turned the final on its head with two wickets in successive deliveries, accounting for Lamb and Chris Lewis. Imran, playing in his last one-day international for Pakistan, took the wicket of Richard Illingworth as Pakistan beat us by 22 runs.

Fairbrother and I were absolutely gutted at the end of it all. There is nothing worse in any sport than to reach a final and to lose, because you have gone to bed on the eve of the match dreaming of glory, hoping that it might be down to you to perhaps take the crucial wicket or hit the winning run, and there is nowhere to hide if you lose.

Losing one World Cup final was bad enough, but now I had lost two and I was realistic enough to know that there may not be another chance for me, and that meant it hurt all the more.

It turned out that my worst fears were confirmed during the 1996 competition, hosted by India, Pakistan and Sri Lanka. The tournament got off to the worst possible start when Australia and West Indies refused to send their teams to Sri Lanka in protest at the Central Bank bombing by the Tamil Tigers less than a month before the tournament began. The Sri Lankans could not guarantee the safety of the Australian and West Indies teams – after much negotiation, Sri Lanka were awarded victories against both teams, which meant they had qualified for the quarter-finals before playing a game. The United Arab Emirates, Kenya and Holland made their debuts in a revamped competition.

Group A comprised Sri Lanka, Australia, West Indies, India, Zimbabwe and Kenya, with Group B consisted of Pakistan, England, New Zealand, Holland, United Arab Emirates and South Africa.

Up until this point, Sri Lanka had been everybody's whipping boys, but they were about to prove that everything had changed. They used Sanath Jayasuriya and Romesh Kaluwithara as opening batsmen, and those two changed the face of one-day cricket forever during that tournament. This was a time when 50 or 60 runs from the first 15 overs was seen as an adequate return, but the Sri Lankans scored 117 in those overs against India and 123 against Kenya. They scored 398 for five against Kenya, a record that stood until 2006.

Their batting was like a juggernaut, so explosive that it didn't really matter what their bowlers did. We lost to New Zealand in our opening match, beat the UAE and Holland, and lost to South Africa and Pakistan. We reached the quarter-finals by the skin of our teeth, but the bad news was that we had to play Sri Lanka in Faisalabad. It would have been hard enough if we had been playing well, but we weren't.

We stumbled to 235 for eight, but then Jayasuriya blew us away as they scored 121 runs in the first 15 overs and we were on our way home. Next, Sri Lanka swept India aside, and then they beat Australia in the final. It was breathtaking to watch and everybody agreed that they were worthy winners and that we would all have to change the way we played one-day cricket or else Sri Lanka would dominate it for years.

I now knew that I'd bowled my last ball in World Cup cricket. During my 103 one-day internationals I scored 690 runs at an average of 16.04, and my best was 67, but you have to remember that I came in towards the end of the innings when it was necessary to throw bat at ball, as is confirmed by my strike rate of 88.83. I took 115 wickets, with a best of 35 for four, and an economy rate of 3.96. I believe that I always gave the one-day team value for money, and the fact that I played so many matches speaks for itself – remember that when I was in my prime there was nothing like the amount of one-day cricket that there is now.

CHAPTER 11
GUESS WHAT? YOU'RE BACK IN

At the end of 1987, England was due to tour Pakistan. I continued to work away at my game, simmering with resentment that a group of selectors who had seen something in me after I had played just one full season of county cricket, had treated me so shabbily just a few weeks later.

And guess what? When the squad was announced, I was back in. I had read about the subcontinent and I had seen pictures on television, but nothing can prepare you for the reality of it.

I enjoyed it because it was different. Boy, was it different. First of all there was the intense heat and humidity – it wasn't a lot of fun running in at full steam, I can tell you. There was also a tremendous amount of poverty, and there was no escaping it because it is in your face almost all the time, other than when we were playing cricket.

Sitting on the team bus heading towards the ground, whether it be in Karachi, Riwalpindi or anywhere else, was a sobering experience. Every time we would come to a halt (which was every few yards), the bus would be surrounded by children begging for money. They had all sorts of injuries and deformities, and there were adults who were just the same, who had probably being begging on the streets from the time they were old enough to do so.

The problem is that the poverty is so widespread that I don't suppose there is anything the authorities can do about it. And life is cheap. Lots of men, women and children die in traffic accidents, but nobody seems to care.

There was also the issue of the food. Now, England take their own chef, who is responsible for cooking all the team's meals. I guess they must go out for the odd meal, but back then we put our fate in the hands of local chefs and local food and spices. The result was that at some stage or other you could be certain that every member of the party would be unwell, and sometimes you had no option to go out and play, no matter how dreadful you felt. It was just one of the perils of touring that part of the world. Everybody loses weight.

For all that, it was an exciting country and I found the people to be very friendly, and they couldn't do enough for us. They always wanted to please you, and would have given you their last grain of rice. Yet again though, most of us felt that the tour went on for too long – none of us wanted to be away from home for three months, having spent the previous winter Down Under, and it was an anti-climax.

There were times when I felt homesick. It is difficult to put your finger on the specifics but there always tends to be one thing that will trigger it, and then you can't wait to climb aboard the plane that will bring you back to Gatwick or Heathrow and the familiarity of an English winter or the early part of an English spring.

The Pakistan public were cricket-mad. At that time in my life, I had never experienced anything quite like it. Mike Gatting was still in charge and although we didn't know it when we arrived in Pakistan, he was to be a central figure in a controversy that very nearly destroyed political relations between the United Kingdom and Pakistan.

This was in the days before neutral umpires, and we always felt that we needed to take 40 wickets to win a Test match in the subcontinent. If you clean-bowled somebody, or there was an obvious edge and the ball was taken by a fielder, there wasn't much the umpire could do but give the batsman out, but leg before wicket (lbw) was a different matter altogether, so we felt that we had to bowl out each player twice in each innings, just to make sure.

Some of the decisions were diabolical. I guess you could have called it cheating, although the umpires would probably say it was nothing more than a hint of local bias. All I can say is that I am delighted we now have neutral umpires and the review system.

There had been tension between the teams in England during the summer, and the sensible thing would have been to sit the respective captains and umpires down before the series began in an effort to clear the air. That would have been the sensible thing, but of course it didn't happen.

We felt that things were always against us.

I have suffered at various times in my career with a bunion, and just before the second Test in Faisalabad it started playing up, so Laurie Brown, the physiotherapist, took me to the hospital, where they offered to treat it – I had serious doubts, so I asked Laurie if he had any needles that would be suitable and he said that he didn't. I decided that I would take some painkillers and wait until I came home to have it looked at.

Anyway, Laurie didn't put up any resistance to my decision. I was ruled out of the game and was named as 12th man. The match took place in early December, but there wasn't a lot of festive spirit. It began when Gatting claimed what everybody thought was a legitimate catch but was overruled by Shakoor Rana, the umpire. Gatts muttered something like: "One rule for one, one for another."

Later, the umpire accused Gatting of cheating as he instructed Bill Athey to take a different fielding position, and that turned out to be the final straw for the England captain. A furious row erupted, with both men shouting and pointing fingers at one another. It was an extraordinary scene, and certainly wasn't something that any of us had seen before, but the England players were right behind Mike and didn't feel he did anything wrong. I still don't.

The following day, Rana refused to take the field until Gatting apologised to him, but Gatts was just as adamant that he wanted Rana to withdraw his cheating accusation.

It had all been blown up out of all proportion and I just thought the whole thing was complete madness. In the end, the Test and County Cricket Board ordered Gatting to apologise so that the Test could resume. Unsurprisingly, he was bitterly unhappy but he agreed to do so in order that we could start playing cricket again.

Then we went off to Lahore and Chris Broad was given out and, I am sorry, but there was just no way under the sun that he was out. He stood his ground and announced that he wasn't going anywhere. "That's blatant cheating," he said. "I am not walking." You have to understand that in cricket, probably more so than in any other sport, the umpire's word is final. If you are given out, you have to go, unless you are playing in a match in which the review system is available. Back in those days, however, there was no review system and players had no right of appeal. The umpire's finger went up and, no matter how unfair or wrong you thought the decision might be, you were expected to leave the field.

As Broad stood his ground, myself and the other England players were on the dressing-room balcony encouraging him to stay where he was.

Eventually Graham Gooch trudged down from the other end and told him he had to go. It remained potentially explosive and it was tough for us because so many terrible decisions went against us. At one point we felt so badly treated that we threatened to quit the tour.

I remember some diplomats becoming involved and trying to smooth over the trouble. We were taken into a room, the door was closed and we were told: "Looks guys, it is important that this tour continues. It is important for kids' cricket back home, and it is important for relations between England and Pakistan as countries."

We felt that we were not being given a fair crack of the whip, and our government was telling us that we had to take it on the chin and get on with it. Never mind the fact that we felt we were being cheated. They said that they were going to pay us some extra money, but this wasn't about money, it was about a sense of fair play. We agreed to carry on, but it simply left a bad taste for the rest of the tour.

There was an incident in the Test in Karachi where I sent down a delivery, the batsman edged it, Gatting caught it. Not out. I was flabbergasted and kicked the ground, muttering to myself that I'd had enough and that I wasn't going to take any more. Gatts had to pull me away.

Pakistan was not the only time I came across umpires whom I considered to be biased. There was another occasion in New Zealand where I was swinging the ball back in quite beautifully and I had Bruce Edgar and John Wright plumb leg-before, went up to appeal. Not out. Not out.

I was so angry that at one point I started bowling close to the stumps so that I could hit the umpire. I was enraged.

You may find this difficult to fathom but despite all the hassle and the bad feeling, I enjoyed touring Pakistan. I bowled pretty well, and I also found the people very friendly, even when all the rubbish was happening. I got to know Wasim Akram and Javed Miandad, and both of them treated me really well. I wasn't surprised that Wasim went out of his way to help me and look after me, but Javed had a bit of a reputation for being somewhat aloof, so it came as a pleasant surprise to discover that he was nothing of the sort.

These were two world-class cricketers and they didn't even need to acknowledge my existence, far less befriend me.

But things were so bad between the two countries that England would not tour Pakistan again until the winter of 2000. There was also a sense that Gatting was living on borrowed time and in 1988 he allegedly had an affair with a barmaid and was sacked as England captain. Many of the team believed the authorities had been looking for an excuse to get rid of him, and this had provided them with the perfect excuse.

A lot of people may remember him purely for the Rana incident, but he was a fine cricketer who stood up for his teammates. His record as England captain may not have been the greatest but you will not hear me say a bad word about him. I also played under Gooch and Mike Atherton for England, and they were all different in their own ways, each one bringing various strengths and weaknesses to the task. For me, though, Gatts was the best of the lot because he always seemed to know the right thing to say or do.

You have to form some kind of relationship with a captain and I felt that I could open up to Gatting, and that he would listen and be able to say the right thing back to me. I don't know what it was, but I guess that I simply trusted the guy. He would always be supportive and would always be there for me.

I always admired and respected Gooch, who was a wonderful cricketer, but I couldn't speak to him in the same way that I was able to with Gatting. Even today, I still see a fair bit of Goochie and I like him a lot, but I still would not be able to open up to him.

He was a tough captain in as much as he practised and trained really hard, and he expected everybody else to do the same, but he would never ask you to do anything that he wasn't prepared to do himself. That suited me because I loved training hard, but there was never a close bond between the two of us.

As far as Athers was concerned, he too was a magnificent batsman. Time and again he held the England innings together, and he often must have felt like it was him against the world. However, the two of us had clashed at Lancashire during pre-season. He had turned up and one of the first things I said to him was: "I don't like students," and he got the wrong end of the stick and assumed I was talking about him. From that point on, we never had the easiest of relationships. What I had actually meant was that if Lancashire were playing a pre-season friendly against a university side then I wanted to beat them, to set us up for the proper contests to come.

We were from totally different backgrounds. I had come straight from school into county cricket and had to work very hard to get where I was, whereas Atherton had gone to university, was known from very early on as FEC (future England captain) and walked straight into the team. There may have been some resentment on my part.

His future was mapped out for him and to be fair to him, he achieved his goals. I suppose his biggest frustration was that, by and large, his England teammates weren't good enough and he suffered many disappointments as captain of his country.

When he was first appointed, the press tried to make a meal of the fact that the two of us didn't get on, but it was never really like that. I am sure that everybody works with certain people whom they respect as colleagues but wouldn't want to mix with socially or regard as friends.

As with Gooch, I found that I couldn't really talk to Athers so instead I would confide in Neil Fairbrother, my Lancashire teammate. I have always felt that it is very important that you have people in your life you can share your feelings with. Throughout my life I have struggled to do that and, as a result, would often bottle things up, which did me no good at all in either my personal or my professional life.

Finding people to trust has always been a big issue for me, and it still is.

CHAPTER 12
TEAM GAMES

Leicestershire had a good team – on paper at least. Our problem was that we simply didn't play as a team, and they also struggled when the England boys were away on international duty. There must also have been a degree of resentment when the likes of myself, David Gower and Peter Willey came back and walked straight into the side, displacing those who had been deputising for us.

After the Ashes tour, Gower stepped down as captain, to be replaced by Willey. One of the first things our new captain said to me was: "Don't you start being like Botham just because you have been with him on tour."

It was a pretty crass thing to say. I had never given anything less than 100% for my county and that wasn't going to change simply because I had been on an England tour. Why would I have changed? If anything, I thought that I had grown up on that trip because I had no choice – I had been thrown in at the deep end after all, playing for my country when I had only expected to be taken along for the ride.

Willey meant well, I am sure he did. He was a hard man but he helped me in my career. He was very black and white, and I respected that. I like to deal with people who leave you in no doubt as to where you stand with them, rather than being nice to your face and then stabbing you in the back the moment you walk away.

He was especially good to me in my first season, and I also figured he was a pretty good captain. But he was definitely harder on me when I came back from Australia than he had been before and what he did not realise or understand was that by dealing with me in that way it was yet another example of me being taken back to my childhood which, as you know by now, I did not enjoy.

I felt threatened and wanted to go back into my shell. Naturally, it also affected my confidence. I know that I deal with that sort of thing really badly – if something in my life looks like it will turn out to be horrible I will become incredibly defensive, and I find it very difficult to communicate effectively and describe what I feel. It is an entirely different matter if I am being subjected to constructive criticism, but Willey had no reason to assume that just because I had shared time with Ian Botham that I would turn out to be a Big-Time Charlie. I was fully aware of my limitations as a cricketer and was also painfully aware of my limitations as a human being.

Willey's comments triggered something within where I felt that the time had come for me to move on, and I also remained deeply concerned about Leicestershire's inability to play as a team, so I resolved to bide my time and wait for the right thing to come along.

During the winter of 1987-88 I toured Pakistan with England and Neil Fairbrother was one of my teammates. If you cut Fairbrother's arm he would bleed Lancashire. He loves the place and he was full of the joys of playing for Lancs.

He took me to one side and said: "Listen Phil, I know that Lancashire would love to have you on board. Clive Lloyd wants you and so does

David Hughes. All you have to do is say the word. Wasim Akram is coming to play with us next season – we are serious about trying to build a good side."

I wanted to play for a successful team, and I wanted to pick up some silverware. Everything that Neil said to me made perfect sense, so I told him I would definitely be interested in joining. I arranged to meet Hughes and promised him that I would sign.

At the beginning of the 1988 season I went to Grace Road and told them I was leaving. Mike Turner said that he didn't want me to go and he actually asked David Gower to have a word with me during a county match at Bristol to see if he could persuade me to stay. My mind was made up though. I was going (I didn't know it then, but I would be back) and so it was that I came to join Lancashire, and now I really couldn't believe my luck. I spent six glorious years at Old Trafford in what was the best spell of my entire career. I actually lost count of the number of trophies we won during that time.

On my first pre-season with Lancs we went to Zimbabwe and I shared a room with Mike Watkinson. Everybody had headed off to somewhere called My Place, which was a restaurant and bar. We were in Harare and in a city like that you are told where you can and can't go. This was meant to be a good place, where we would probably be able to hook up with some of the Zimbabwean players.

Mike and I stopped a taxi. "Can you take us to My Place please?"

"Yeah, yeah, no problem."

We were driving for ages, and Mike and I were getting a bit anxious, especially when we realised we were in the shanty town. The next thing we knew, he pulled up and said: "Here you are guys, my place." He had driven us to his own home.

"No, no, no mate. My Place, the restaurant in Harare."

"Oh, My Place! Right then, let's go."

You couldn't make it up.

CHAPTER 13
YOU'RE THE DADDY

A great deal happened to me during my years at Old Trafford. For starters, I bought my first proper home, a terraced house in Hale. At this point I was still going out with Emma Hobson, and she had come up with me. We stayed with Neil Fairbrother and his wife, Audrey. Steve O'Shaunessy, who played for Lancashire and is now an umpire, took me to look at the house and just as I was about to leave Neil's house, Audrey asked if I was taking Emma with me. "Why?" I asked. There was no question that this was going to be anything other than my home.

On our way back to Leicester, things were very awkward. I suddenly realised what I had done, and it was shortly after this that our relationship came to an end.

I was still young (just 22 when I started playing for them) and, of course, I was still single. But not for long.

My first season with Lancashire went pretty well, I made new friends within the dressing room and got to know the best places to go in and around Manchester. There was a game during that first summer that we won very easily, which was not unusual back then. It meant we had an extra day off so a few of us went out, including Patrick Patterson, the West Indies fast bowler.

We ended up in a wine bar based in a Manchester hotel and had a few drinks. We'd had a great win and it wasn't long before the champagne came out; well we had three or four days off, so it wasn't a problem.

The next thing I knew was that we had been joined by three attractive girls, and we were all having a laugh and a joke together. Needless to say, by the end of the evening, I was absolutely hammered again, but I managed to stop a taxi and persuade the driver to take me home. Alongside me was one of the girls.

We ended up back at my place, where I put some music on, and we both finished up in bed, where she spent the night. I woke up the next morning, not especially proud of myself, and told her I had to go into work, but offered to drop her off and then went training to shake off the effects of the night before.

A few days later, riddled with guilt at the way I had treated this girl, I climbed into my car and tried to find where she lived because I wanted to apologise, but I couldn't remember exactly where it was I had dropped her off, so that was that.

Then, at the end of the year I went on a tour of India and met Nicola McDonald. We were in Mumbai (or Bombay as it was back then) and she was on holiday with her parents. She worked for Gulf Air, the airline. The team had been due to move to another venue but there was a delay with our transport so we ended up staying in the hotel for an additional night, the same hotel Nicola and her parents were staying.

I went down to the bar to have a drink in the evening, she was there with her parents and we started chatting and immediately hit it off. One of the things that always helped me get through a tour was listening to music but inevitably you get bored of listening to the same old stuff so I asked her if she had anything that we could swap. It turned out that she did, and then we exchanged phone numbers.

When I got back from India I phoned her and we started seeing each other, even though she lived in Burton on Trent and I was in Hale. She came up to stay with me a few times and I soon realised that our relationship was developing and that we had fallen in love with each other, so she moved in with me.

Maybe I was ready to settle down after all.

But the 1989 season had a huge shock in store for me, and it had nothing to do with my cricket. We were playing a match at Old Trafford and were batting when the dressing room attendant walked in and told me that there was somebody on the phone for me. I picked it up and a girl's voice on the other end said: "You won't remember me but I've got some news for you."

I hadn't a clue who she was or what she was talking about. "Go on then," I said. "Tell me."

"You've got a daughter."

"What?"

"Yes, that's right. You've got a daughter."

I was dumbstruck.

"No way, that's not right," I eventually replied. "You are taking the mickey."

"I wish I was."

With that, I put the phone down, but she rang again straight away and repeated her claim. I told her it was rubbish, and then I phoned my solicitor and told him there was some woman on the scene claiming that I had fathered her child. I was convinced she had targeted me because I was somebody in the public eye and she maybe figured that she could get some money out of me.

The next thing was that she turned up at the ground with the baby. I was only 23 and I looked at this little girl and said: "No, no way. This is not right. This has nothing to do with me. My solicitor will deal with it."

Blood tests were arranged and the results proved that the baby was mine – the mother was the girl I had slept with the previous summer after meeting her in the Manchester wine bar. Eventually we went to court to sort out maintenance, but I wasn't interested in bonding in any way with this little girl. It was not my proudest hour. The girl was called Amber and her mother was named Deborah.

Nicola was terribly hurt by all of this, but I stressed to her that what had happened between Deborah and I had been before I met Nicola. She wanted to be the first woman to provide me with a child so it was a big deal for her, and of course I understand that.

Where she was incredibly good though was in dealing with all the practicalities, right down to sorting out the direct debit for the monthly maintenance payment. I went through all sorts of different emotions. For me, at one point it was as if Amber didn't exist.

The story was eventually sold to *The Sun* newspaper, which disappointed me greatly, and she was branded by them as a love child. She was not a love child – I had a one-night stand with Deborah, something that I am not proud of. And I was single, just as Deborah was – we were both old enough to make our own choices and decisions.

The whole thing hit me very hard. As much as I tried to put it to the back of my mind, and believe me, I did, I could not get away from the fact that there was a girl out there who was my daughter and she had been born in circumstances that I would never have planned or condoned. As she grew up, I had nothing to do with her, apart from making sure that her mother received the maintenance payments on time every month.

As time went by, I found it increasingly difficult to live with the fact that I had no involvement in Amber's life. Whenever the subject came up, it was like a knife being delivered to my heart. I don't know if it was because of the relationship I had with my father, but the whole thing nearly destroyed me.

"She doesn't exist, she doesn't exist, she doesn't exist..."

But she did exist. She does exist. Thank God, we have all grown up and I do now have some contact with her. Amber has grown up to be a wonderful girl, for which her mother must take 100% of the credit.

Amber now lives in Manchester and has a boyfriend, and I see her from time to time and am proud to play even a small part in her life.

The knowledge that I was a father definitely contributed to my decision to settle down with Nicola. I was aware that there were rumours flying around that I was turning into some kind of wild child, which was never the case, but I knew that the England hierarchy wouldn't be happy until I was married and had children in a rather more orthodox manner. I should never have been influenced by them.

In my view, I got the balance right between my private, professional and social life. You will probably have worked out by now that although I like to have nice things around me, I don't go in for showing off or being ostentatious.

Nicky and I had talked about getting married, but then I was called out to join the Ashes tour in 1990. I arranged to meet my financial adviser before I left and said: "I've had this England call-up but we are thinking of getting married and I thought we would just do it in a registry office, I can fly out to Australia and Nicola can fly out later in the tour to join me and we can make it our honeymoon."

It all became a bit of a rush, but we did get married in Burton on Trent. Her parents were there but mine weren't because I didn't want to ask my Dad and it would have been unfair to ask Mum to come on her own. It was just too much hassle, and I figured I could tell them later. It was another instance of me failing to face up to things, another example of my insecurity. I regret it now and I also regret not giving Nicola the big wedding I know she wanted.

After the wedding, I had to sign all sorts of things over to her so that she could look after them while I was out of the country. Mentally, I wasn't right at that time. The more I think about it now, the more certain I am that what happened with Deborah pushed me towards Nicola and backed me into a corner when I felt I had no option but to propose. I am not blaming anybody else for this – these were my decisions, and I was the one who had to face the consequences although, ultimately, Nicola would have to face them too.

I loved her and she loved me, and that is why we got married. We also decided that we would try for a baby straight away, but I had to join the England team in Australia and when I told them all that I had just got married they all took the mickey out of me, but I didn't care, and I was delighted when she phoned me and told me that she was pregnant.

I was thrilled, and all the more so when Alexandra was born. She was a beautiful baby and I should have been the happiest man alive but instead I was thinking: "Gosh, I have a wife and a daughter. I am too young to be married and have all this responsibility. I should be giving my entire focus to my cricket."

That sounds awful, but I am sure that anybody who has ever played professional sport will know precisely what I mean. The whole thing was a massive shock to my system. Instead of going back to my own place and having it to myself, here I was going back to a family, and I wasn't ready for it. Nobody held a gun to my head, nobody forced me to ask Nicola to marry me and nobody forced me to have a baby, but it was tough.

It was also tough on them because the nature of the way I earned my living meant that I spent a lot of time away from home, either with Lancashire or with England. I missed out on a great deal of Alexandra growing up, although Nicola brought her out to New Zealand when I was on tour and while she was there she took her first unaided steps, and it was a real thrill to see that. I came back from training one day and she walked across the room to greet me.

I toured a great deal in those days and I found that when I came home I didn't really have a proper relationship with either my wife or my daughter – it was almost as if we were strangers to one another, and that was hardly surprising. The advantage was that every time I came home, it was all fresh, but then I had to face up to the realities, to the problems that Nicola had faced while I had been away. This needed to be done, that needed to be repaired.

Thankfully, I had my cricket. And boy, was I blessed in that respect. I used to look around at my Lancashire teammates and wonder what I had done to deserve a place in the same team. For instance, there was Wasim Akram, who was one of the most gifted cricketers it has been my privilege to know.

He was a match-winner for Lancashire and for Pakistan but he was very unusual in that everything seemed to be so natural. He never appeared to have to work hard on his bowling or batting. Of course he made his name as one of the world's best fast bowlers, but he was also an explosive batsman, in the style of Botham, and he could turn a game with a quickfire burst of runs before getting the ball in his hands and blasting out the opposition's top order. I was lucky enough to open the bowling with him and we developed a good partnership that opposing sides did not relish coming up against.

And if I wasn't bowling in partnership with Wasim, the man at the other end would be Patrick Patterson, who was one of the world's fastest bowlers. Then there was Neil Fairbrother, who was a tremendous batsman and a real livewire, a bundle of nervous energy.

It wasn't all plain sailing. One day, an argument began in the dressing room between myself and Michael Atherton – neither of us can remember how it began. I was holding a bat while Athers was sitting next to a tray of sausage rolls, which he began to throw at me. I let loose with the bat, but missed the sausage roll and caught Neil Fairbrother right on the bridge of his nose – we were in the middle of a match, and Neil had to sit out the next session.

I would never have considered myself and Athers to be bosom buddies but when he was appointed England captain he had no hesitation in picking me, and I believe that marked him out as a special individual.

Almost from the very first day, I knew that moving to Lancashire was a great move for me. We had a decent championship side, but it was in the one-day game that we really came into our own. On our day, we were unbeatable, and we had many great days. Not only that, but we had fun.

I remember playing a championship game against Middlesex at Lord's and they had a decent side that included Mike Gatting, John Emburey and the great West Indies batsman Desmond Haynes, so they were never a pushover. I opened the bowling for Lancashire with Patrick Patterson, starting at the Nursery End before eventually switching to the Pavilion End – it's an odd thing but I never really enjoyed bowling from the Pavilion End, even though it was from there that I got my Test-best seven for 70 against Sri Lanka.

Middlesex had made steady progress in the morning and we came in for lunch and I looked down at my trousers and realised that there were a couple of holes in the legs and several grass stains from where I had been diving around in the field. I thought to myself: "I cannot possibly go back out at Lord's dressed like this. It just isn't right."

I normally took two pairs of trousers to every match, one for bowling, the other for batting, but on this occasion the only pair that I had with me were the ones I was wearing, and they really were looking sorry for themselves. My good mate Neil Fairbrother offered to lend me a pair of his trousers. Fine, expect that you need to know Neil is a good four or five inches shorter than me.

So I put the trousers on and they finished around the top of my socks. "You can't go out looking like that," said Neil.

"Listen mate, they are white and they are clean and are a damn sight more presentable than the ones I was wearing. It will be fine. Thanks a lot buddy."

I went out in the afternoon and bowled as quickly as I had done for a long time. You can draw your own conclusions from that – maybe it was because I wanted to take a load of wickets and get off the field as quickly as possible, or maybe it was because they were a bit tight around the nether regions! I ended up taking seven wickets for 20 runs, producing my career-best figures, and both Gatting and Haynes commented afterwards that I had bowled faster than Patterson, who was reckoned to be the quickest on the planet at that time. And it was all achieved in Fairbrother's borrowed pants!

There are not many bowlers who are able to say that they produced both their best Test and county figures at Lord's, but I can. I was so proud of that achievement that whenever I looked like I might be in with a chance of bettering it, I didn't want to take another wicket. It may sound strange, but anybody who has played first-class cricket will understand. My only regret was that I was unable to score my best with the bat at Lord's – I scored the odd half century there, but never came close to making a hundred.

The approach between Lancashire and Leicestershire was very different. At Grace Road I felt that I was playing for a club side, but at Old Trafford everything was done in a very professional way although we were encouraged to enjoy our cricket. Everything was taken care of for the players at Lancashire, so all we had to worry about was getting out to the middle and doing what we were being paid to do.

At Leicestershire, there was a deal with Sketchley's, the dry cleaners, but most of the guys used to take their whites home and wash them; at Lancs, after a day's play we would leave our whites and when we returned the next day everything was washed and pressed. Simple things like that made a difference.

When I left Grace Road I was earning £10,000 a season, and my first contract for Lancashire was for £18,000. But let's put this in perspective – when I moved to Lancs in 1988 I was 22 years old and a full England international. Of course the money was better, but it could hardly be described as a fortune and it certainly wasn't my primary motivation. As I have already said, I wanted to win things.

David Hughes, the captain, was in a class by himself when it came to man management. He was one of those guys who knew what to say and when to say it, and we all wanted to play our hearts out for him.

At the start of every season we would all set one of our goals as getting to Lord's for another one-day final – every time we did it, we got a new suit, and we were all very fashion-conscious and wanted to look our best at all times.

It wasn't just about the cricket or the suits though. Our wives and girlfriends would come down to London with us and after the game we would all head off to Stringfellow's nightclub – and you only really wanted to go in there if you had won the trophy. It was a big deal for us all, so every season we made sure that we got to a Lord's final. And make no mistake about it, the fans loved their big day out every bit as much as we did.

Of course it helped that we had such a wonderful squad of players and that all of us possessed tremendous self-belief – you can't get to the top in sport unless you have that kind of faith in your own ability.

In 1990 we had a memorable year, winning both the Benson and Hedges Cup and the NatWest Cup, which meant we went to Lord's twice.

Sadly, we never quite won the County Championship, although we came close several times – the reason for that was that so many of the players spent large parts of the season on Test duty. It still seems inconceivable to me that Lancs haven't won the championship since 1950.

I am not especially superstitious but if I took a load of wickets or hit a big score with the bat while wearing a particular set of whites, I would always make sure that they were cleaned and ready to wear the next time around. And I always made sure that I put my left pad on first and my left glove first – don't ask me why. I also hated other people touching my gear. Don't pick up my bat – it's mine. I was always very organised, with everything where it should be. I am not talking OCD; I am talking about being properly prepared, so I could not get my head around cricketers who would leave their stuff strewn all over the changing room.

Jack Russell, the England wicketkeeper, was obsessive about his tatty old white hat, which lasted him from his debut in 1981 until he retired in 2004. He refused to wear the official coloured one-day sun hat in South Africa, with a compromise reached only when Russell said he would put it on if he could wear his own underneath. On another occasion in the West Indies, he washed it, put it in an oven to dry and forgot about it. He remembered about it in the nick of time, saving it before it was completely destroyed.

His gloves and helmet had also seen better days, but he wouldn't wear anything else.

The truth is that he was a scruffy so-and-so, but what a fantastic character and a great man to have on your side. Russell would often get through 20 cups of tea a day. He used to dip the tea bag in once, add plenty of milk, then hang it on a nail ready for subsequent use. In the final Test of the 1989 Ashes series (against Australia) at The Oval, Derek Pringle claimed that Jack used the same bag for all five days. For lunch, Russell would eat two Weetabix soaked for exactly eight minutes in milk, and a mashed banana. For dinner, steak and chips or chicken without skin was a favourite meal - Russell once spent every night of a Test at a Chinese restaurant in Perth, ordering cashew chicken: without the cashews.

We shared a room in Pakistan, by which time Jack was really into his painting – he was, and is, a brilliant artist. His stuff was scattered all over our room and in the end I drew a line down the middle and told him he could have all the space on one side of it and could make as much of a mess as he wanted within, but the rest was mine and had to be kept clean and tidy. "If any of your stuff comes over here, I will throw it straight back," I told him.

On days off, he would disappear with his brushes, his paints and his easel and go away and paint. While we were on tour, I was lying fast asleep on the physio's bench in Faisalabad and Jack sketched me.

CHAPTER 14
REBEL, REBEL

Because of apartheid, South Africa had been kicked out of international cricket. The message was clear – until you start considering black players for selection to the national side, no Test-playing nation will travel to South Africa or invite them to tour. I suppose it must have been a devastating blow, and it also meant that the world was deprived of seeing some great players in action.

In 1982, Graham Gooch had led an England XI on a one-month tour of South Africa. With the exception of Ian Botham, it was advertised as pretty much a full-strength side and they played thee unofficial Tests and three one-day games. The Springboks, captained by Mike Procter, won the 'Test' series 1-0 and the one-day series 3-0.

Gooch's team included Geoff Boycott, Dennis Amiss, Derek Underwood, Peter Willey, John Lever, Chris Old and Alan Knott, and I understand that they were all fairly handsomely rewarded for their efforts. All the rebels were banned for three years, ending the international careers of more than half the team, including Boycott.

In subsequent years, Sri Lanka, West Indies and Australia rebel teams toured South Africa. There was always a tremendous amount of publicity and players were duly banned, but as most were coming to the end of

Martin and Sybil DeFreitas, my parents, on their wedding day

Hair-raising – well, I thought that I looked pretty cool

Family affair – I played cricket for Sudbury Court alongside my brother, Faron. I am third from the left, he is second from the right

A young Defreitas in country finery, its my blazer and whites from my 1st tour to Australia in 1986/7

Walking out to bat at Grace Road in 1985, knowing I was about to face the bowling of Ian Botham

Above: Here I am with Ken Higgs, left, and Ted Dexter, being presented with the Websters Yorkshire Bitter Fast-Bowling Performance of the Month Trophy after taking 13 wickets against Essex

Right: Fancy dress is part of the tradition of an England tour at Christmas. I agreed to be Diana Ross, but drew the line at shaving off the moustache. The "cat" next to me is Sir Ian Botham

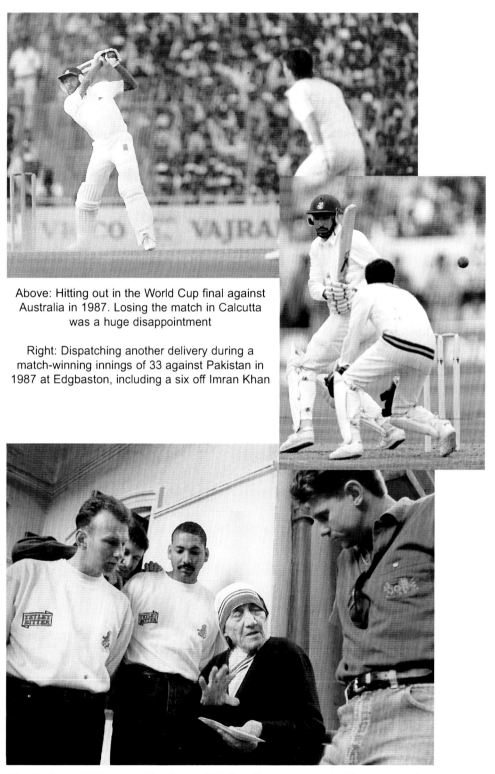

Above: Hitting out in the World Cup final against Australia in 1987. Losing the match in Calcutta was a huge disappointment

Right: Dispatching another delivery during a match-winning innings of 33 against Pakistan in 1987 at Edgbaston, including a six off Imran Khan

The thrill of a lifetime – getting to meet Mother Teresa, a wonderful woman and an inspiration. Neil Fairbrother, left, and Robin Smith, right, were also entranced by her

Left: My old mucker Gladstone Small congratulates me after I take a wicket for England

Below: 13 I had some great times with Lancashire. Here we are celebrating after winning the National League

With my Lancashire teammates, who did the double, including Michael Atherton, David Hughes, Neil Fairbrother and Patrick Patterson. That's me in the front row on the extreme right

Botham makes the long walk back after being bowled by me in the Lords Final when we beat Worcestershire in the Benson and hedges final

England captain Graham Gooch does the honours as we meet Prince Phillip at Lord's

Above: With the incomparable David Hughes after winning the NatWest Trophy for Lancashire in 1990

Left: Raised high by Paul Allott and Gehan Mendis after being named man of the match for taking five wickets as we beat Northants in the NatWest Trophy final in 1990

Left: You've got to admit, it wasn't a bad bowling action, was it?

Below: My last County Championship game for Leicestershire, with wicketkeeper Paul Nixon

With my daughter Alexandra and a pair of feathered friends

Above: With Sir Trevor McDonald and my good Friend Peter Evans

Right: Happy families – here I am with Barnaby, Rafferty and Katie

their careers and were being paid huge sums of money to go to South Africa, they were not unduly troubled.

The West Indian teams engendered the greatest controversy. Was it a case of black players showing the white population of South Africa that they were their equals, or had they sold themselves out? I suppose there was some truth to both arguments.

Towards the end of 1989 I was approached by Ali Bacher, who had organised the other tours, and was asked if I would consider joining another England rebel tour of South Africa. I am sure he felt that it would be something of a coup for him if he could persuade a coloured Englishman to join the party.

I had played a Test against Australia at Headingley in 1989 and was dropped again, so I was pretty disillusioned. All that I had ever wanted to do was to play for my country. What did I have to do? The frustration was building up within me as I kicked my heels at home, wondering what I was doing wrong.

Bacher told me that Mike Gatting, my former England captain, had signed up, along with Tim Robinson, Paul Jarvis, Neil Foster, Graham Dilley, Bruce French and Chris Broad.

Even before Bacher contacted me, I was beginning to feel like I'd had enough with England, so I was definitely receptive to anything he had to say. I arranged to meet him at Piccadilly station in Manchester and he wasted little time in getting down to business. Bacher showed me a figure he had written on a piece of paper and told me it was what I would be paid if I agreed to join the tour – I felt like I was being paid peanuts by England so when I looked down and saw the figure '£75,000' I was blown away. He also told me that Roland Butcher, another coloured player, had agreed to play.

I knew that if I signed up to join the tour I would be banned from playing for England, but at that point I didn't care. The situation in South Africa was the last thing on my mind – I was angry with England, really angry.

"Yes, Ali, I will go." I was going to be in South Africa for less than two months, earning all this money. It seemed like a no-brainer to me.

Then I went home and started thinking about the consequences of my actions. I had acted in haste, agreed to something when I was still very angry with England. As I considered things, I came to the conclusion that I had made a mistake, and that I couldn't go after all, no matter how much money I was being paid. Playing for my country was too important to me.

But before I could contact Bacher and tell him that I had changed my mind, the story broke in the media, and a big thing was made of the fact that I was sticking two fingers up at England. To see it in black and white was something of a shock, especially when people started approaching me and saying stuff like: "You are going to South Africa? You do know that means you are probably sacrificing the rest of your England career, don't you?"

It was one thing to agree to something in the heat of the moment, but it was something else altogether to have people I respected pointing it out to me.

I didn't know it, but after the story broke, Lancashire started receiving lots of hate mail addressed to me. Thankfully, they guessed what it was and made sure I didn't get any of it, but by now I was only concerned with extricating myself from this impossible situation. "What have I done?" I asked myself. "Do I really want to throw away my England future?"

One day I was given a copy of a tabloid newspaper by one of my Lancashire teammates. "I think you should read this Phil," he said.

There was an article in which two prominent coloured British athletes said that they were so disgusted with me that they wouldn't piss on me if they passed me and I was on fire. Suddenly, it hit home. The whole thing was horrendous and, yet again, here was somebody who didn't know me, who hadn't a clue what I had been through with England, expressing their views about me in an incredibly hurtful way. Of course, I know how the media works, and the athletes in question might well have been misquoted, or may have had words put into their mouths by a clever journalist looking for a controversial story.

By this point my family were being subjected to some pretty horrendous stuff, including being threatened, and I was more or less living in hiding. My county teammates knew how I felt about my treatment by England and most of them just shrugged their shoulders and said: "If that's what you want to do, go ahead and do it."

But I had to find a way out, and the more I read about what was going on in South Africa, the more it repelled me. Apartheid was an appalling thing, and it was obvious to any right-minded person that it was wrong. I would play no part in anything that was going to help perpetuate it, and playing cricket in South Africa was essentially saying that it was all right when I knew it wasn't. I realised that many of the other guys who had signed up probably felt their careers were coming to an end and that the money was important to them, but for me it wasn't a price worth paying.

I contacted Ali Bacher and told him that I'd changed my mind and that I wasn't going, and then it emerged that Roland Butcher had also said no. The sense of relief I felt was palpable.

Bacher announced the full squad during the fourth Test of the Ashes series in England and players who were in both squads were immediately discarded, which allowed the likes of Mike Atherton and Devon Malcolm to make their debuts.

As it turned out, the rebel tour was a financial disaster for Bacher. South Africa began the long and slow process of dismantling apartheid, the African National Congress was given legal status once more and Nelson Mandela was finally released from prison. As for the rebel tour matches, they attracted huge protests in South Africa and nobody cared that the home side won the only 'Test' and the one-day series 3-1. International cricket was introduced to the shape of things to come, however, when Allan Donald took eight wickets for 59 in the 'Test'.

When apartheid was finally dismantled, I found it somewhat ironic that one of the athletes who had been so quick to condemn me was one of the first to head out there to run, with a lot of money at stake. People who were happy to pass judgment on me without asking me for my opinion or engaging me in conversation were suddenly prepared to go there.

I am not saying that the rebel tours were the right way to go, but they did focus the world's attention on what was happening in South Africa, and they may even have played a part in extra pressure being exerted on the government.

But events in South Africa were the least of my concerns – or so I thought. It is funny how things work out, but I would end up heading to South Africa and seeing its problems for myself.

CHAPTER 15
KIWI FRUITS

If you look at the Test records of most players, you will find that there is one opponent against whom they thrive. For me, it was New Zealand. I haven't the first idea why that should be, but it may be something to do with the fact that whenever I faced them I had usually been given a decent run in the side.

After the tour of Pakistan in 1987, we came home for a month or so and then headed off to New Zealand early in 1988, and I played against the Kiwis twice, in February and March, at Christchurch and Wellington. I only took four wickets in those matches and didn't score a lot of runs, but I was bowling well.

Next came three Tests against the West Indies in England, at Trent Bridge, Old Trafford and The Oval and once again I only managed to bag a few wickets.

I didn't play for England again until June 1989, when Australia arrived, hungry for revenge. It was the start of their revival, and they gave us the runaround for most of that summer. I only played in the Test at Headingley, and it was a match that is best forgotten. My three wickets cost 216 runs and guess what? I was dropped again.

I was surprised to be chosen to travel to the West Indies in 1990 and played in the Tests at Bridgetown, where I picked up five wickets, and St John's, where I scored 21 in the first innings, a duck in the second and only picked up one wicket.

And that was the way of it. In the side for a couple of games, and then out again.

In June 1990, I took six wickets against New Zealand at Trent Bridge and when we faced them at Lord's I went wicketless but I did manage to score 38 runs in our first innings. At the end of the year we were back Down Under for another Ashes series against Australia, and it was a major surprise to me when I was included in the squad.

I sat out the start of the series and was called in for the Boxing Day Test in Melbourne. It was all very different from four years earlier. Now, it was Australia whose star was in the ascendancy. It wasn't a great Test for me, but I did perform much better in Adelaide, almost a month later. I made 45 in the first innings and was unbeaten on 19 in the second, and chipped in with five wickets. Another three followed in Perth.

And then it was back to England to receive the West Indies in 1991 and there was a rare occurrence for me – I got to play all five Tests, at Headingley, Lord's, Trent Bridge, Edgbaston and The Oval. It had been a long time since I had felt part of the set-up, but that summer I felt like I belonged and it showed in my bowling.

It is worth reflecting for a moment on the West Indies team. The bowling attack was led by Malcolm Marshall, the man I regard as the best fast bowler of them all, and alongside him were Curtly Ambrose, Courtney Walsh and Patrick Patterson who, for a time, was the fastest bowler in the world. When you consider how quick and accurate these guys were, it was a wonder that they ever lost a Test although, to be fair, they didn't lose many.

What was it like to face them? On a hard, fast wicket it was frightening, really frightening, especially as a lower-order batsman. Normally, by the time I came to the crease cracks would have started to appear in the wicket and you could never be absolutely certain where the ball was going to go, but you sure as heck didn't want to be hit by it. It is a source of wonder to me that certain batsmen seemed to thrive against these bowlers. The other thing was that I would often go in to face them just about the time when the new ball was due, so you might have a few overs facing a ball that was coming to the end of its life and find it easy enough to survive and score a few runs.

Then the new ball would arrive, you would take guard, look around and realise the keeper was standing miles back and there were umpteen slips in place – before the new cherry was released, you just knew that it was coming towards your head. In those circumstances, it was quite tricky to bat positively.

Let's put things into some sort of perspective here. Marshall played 81 Tests over 13 years and claimed 376 wickets, including four 10-wicket match hauls (he also scored 10 Test fifties), Walsh played 132 Tests over 17 years and took 519 wickets, including 10 wickets in a match three times, and Ambrose, all 6ft 7in of him, played 98 Tests over 12 years and took 405 wickets – he also managed three 10-wicket test hauls.

And there was no let-up. Two of them would bowl their spells at you and if you were fortunate enough to see them off, you would then have to face two more.

Mark Ramprakash made his England debut in that 1991 series. He would survive for more than an hour, getting to 20-odd and all that it served to do was make the West Indians even more determined to throw the kitchen sink at him – they had collectively made up their minds that they were going to make life as difficult as possible for him.

Ramps was a batsman who liked to play attractive, attacking shots and it was to his credit that he curbed his natural instincts and put the anchor down, but they kept getting him out in the twenties. He showed tremendous guts, courage and determination against the best bowling attack in the world, and how did the selectors reward him? Of course, they dropped him.

It wasn't a lot easier bowling at them either – Viv Richards, Gordon Greenidge, Desmond Haynes, Richie Richardson, Carl Hooper, Jeff Dujon, Gus Logie were all world class batsmen. If one or two of them failed, it was inevitable that somebody else would step up to the mark, and they all had the ability to turn a game on its head very quickly because they could compile big scores in double-quick time.

A young left-handed batsman who loved to play extravagant shots had just broken into the team as well. You may have heard of him – his name was Brian Lara, and he was to make England's bowlers suffer many, many times. He scored 501 for Warwickshire against Durham in 1994 as well as 400 not out against England at Antigua in 2004 – fortunately, I had long stopped playing international cricket by then.

Back in 1991, however, it was yours truly who was making hay against the tourists. I took eight wickets at Headingley, Graham Gooch scored a wonderful 154 and we won by 115 runs. I took three each at Lord's, which ended in a weather-affect draw, and Trent Bridge, where we lost, and five at Edgbaston, where we lost heavily. At Trent Bridge I struck a beautiful unbeaten 55 which, at that point, was my best batting performance for my country.

The final Test was played at The Oval and we went into it trailing 2-1. I took three more wickets but Phil Tufnell, who had been recalled, was the hero with his six wickets for 25 from 14.3 overs turning the game on its head and allowing us to win by five wickets and draw the series.

I considered it a true privilege to have played against that wonderful West Indies team, all the more so because we were able to give them a real run for their money. One of my abiding memories is of the Lord's Test. I bowled to Viv Richards and he played and missed, and I was quite pleased with myself when the same thing happened with the next delivery. And then I let go of the next and he smashed it straight over the scoreboard for six.

Against West Indies, I always felt that if I played well then I would earn respect from them, and Viv's six was his way of telling me that although I had bowled him two cracking deliveries, if I strayed from the perfect line and length by any margin, however small, then I would be watching the ball being hit for a boundary. Those were the sort of contests that brought out the very best in me – and in the likes of Richards.

Some bowlers dreaded running in to Viv, but I enjoyed it. If you could work out a way to get out the best batsman in world cricket then it surely said something about you. For me, it was a test of character, and it kept me focused. You also knew that if you got him, then next up would be Haynes or Greenidge, so you couldn't relax for a second. Of course there were days when you came off second best, but it was the way you handled those days that defined the cricketer you were.

I would hold up my hands and say: "Well played." But inside I swore that I would get them next time, and it became a motivation. I became friends with the likes of Viv, Courtney and Curtly, and I was also close to Malcolm Marshall – everybody involved in cricket was stunned when he died of colon cancer in 1999, aged just 41. He was a universally popular man who left his mark on everybody who came into contact with him.

As with the Australians, we would go into the West Indies' dressing room at the end of the day and I would always sit next to Viv, Curtly or Courtney and just listen to what they had to say, trying to absorb knowledge and work out what it was that made them tick and whether I could adapt it to my game.

I would never say anything but would just sit there in awe. In the main, they spoke about cricket, and on one occasion Marshall and Haynes were involved in a discussion and got so excited that they started talking really quickly – they may as well have been using a foreign language as I couldn't understand a word. Those were special days.

At the end of August 1991, we played a one-off Test against Sri Lanka, who was then an emerging force in the sport. The match was played at Lord's, which is my favourite ground, somewhere that I love playing. It has a special atmosphere and so much history. My wonderful summer continued, and I was on top of my game. This was a decent Sri Lanka side and you had to bowl well to take wickets against them.

We dismissed them in the first innings for 222 and I finished with career-best figures of seven for 70. My only disappointment with that Test was that I didn't finish it with 10 wickets, as I had certainly bowled well enough. Instead I had to make do with 'only' taking eight, but it was good enough to get my name on the honours board – this is something that is reserved for players who take five wickets in a Test at Headquarters or score a century. I thought to myself: "Do you know what Phil? It probably doesn't ever get any better than this." I have still got the ball – the problem is that I put it in a box with a load of other cricket balls with which I took at least five wickets, and now I am not sure which one it is. My sons will get those balls when they are old enough to appreciate what they mean, and they will be able to do whatever they want with them. One of the things that made that Lord's Test even better for me was that Phil Tufnell, my old mate from the MCC groundstaff days, was also in the England team for that match.

I never did want to better those figures – I reckon that most English cricketers would say the same thing; that they would want to produce their best batting or bowling performances at the home of cricket. It meant a huge amount to me.

I was flying, and I didn't want that international season to end, but I had to wait until January 1992, when we flew to New Zealand, to get going again. I bagged a couple of wickets in Christchurch, six in Auckland and was wicketless in Wellington but, once again, I felt that I had bowled consistently and that with a little more luck then I could have picked up a lot more wickets.

Pakistan were the visitors to England in the summer of 1992 and this time I took seven wickets in two Tests against them, at Edgbaston and Lord's.

CHAPTER 16
TORTURED SOUL

One of the most naturally gifted cricketers I ever saw was Chris Lewis, who attended the same school as me in London. He was a natural athlete who looked superb when he was bounding in to send down one of his hostile deliveries. And when he batted, there were times where you felt he could turn a game around in the blink of an eye, such was the destructive power of his hitting.

I suppose the two of us had a lot more in common than our school. We both grew up in the same way, which is to say that neither of us had a silver spoon in our mouths. But at some point in your life, you have to make choices – there will be a split in the road and you know that if you follow one way then all should be okay; equally, you know that if you take the other, it could lead you into some very dark and dangerous places.

For the most part, I believe that I made the correct decisions when it came to those choices. If Chris had done the same, there is no telling what he might have achieved in cricket.

We played together for the Middlesex Under-25 side and then he joined me at Leicestershire. It should have been the making of him.

Throughout his career people always said that he had underachieved. "For such a talented lad, he should be taking more wickets, scoring more runs, winning more games for his team." He must have got sick of hearing and reading it. Yes, he did pull out of the occasional game, saying that he was suffering from migraine attacks – in his defence, anybody who has ever had a really severe migraine will know that the last place you want to be is outside in the sun. When you throw in the effect of running in for countless overs, well I think it makes it easier to understand why he couldn't continue playing. And despite everything that followed, I prefer to give him the benefit of the doubt and believe that he was telling the truth. About the migraines at any rate.

I felt sorry for him. He was a warm, pleasant individual who needed some guidance. Chris needed a comforting arm around him.

Lewis made his Test debut in 1990 against New Zealand and played his last Test match six years later against Pakistan. He played 32 Tests and 53 one-day internationals in a career that was punctuated by highs and lows. There was a fabulous century against India in Madras in 1993 on his 25th birthday, but then there was a Test in the West Indies the following year when he shaved his head and then spent a day in the field without a hat or sunscreen and ended up suffering from sunstroke. *The Sun* newspaper labelled him 'the prat without a hat', and it was difficult to argue with.

On another occasion he turned up late for a Test at The Oval claiming he'd had a puncture and had been delayed because he had to change the wheel. Perhaps something ought to be clarified here. Some of you will know that the team all stayed at the same hotel together, and you may wonder what on earth Chris was doing driving to the ground by himself. In those days that is how things were done – we didn't all get on a coach and travel to and from the ground together. Now I don't know what happened to him that day – it is possible that he slept in and was too embarrassed to admit it

He was always a controversial character, once claiming that three England teammates had taken money to fix the result of a match. He never named the players and the claim was never substantiated. Unsurprisingly, fellow players shunned him after that and he was jeered by spectators wherever he played and so, at the age of 32, he quit the game.

He reached his lowest point in 2009 when he was jailed for 13 years for attempting to smuggle liquid cocaine valued at more than £140,000 into Britain. It was hidden in fruit juice tins in a cricket bag.

On the face of it, if you are charged, appear in court and are found guilty, then you have to face the consequences. But I am very reluctant to judge the man until I hear what he has to say. There are two sides to every story. Like myself, Chris was very insecure and it seems that he was easily led too. I don't know the full circumstances but to get to that state he must have been in a very bad place, and I don't mind admitting that I feel sorry for the man.

When people are calling for help, we need to get to them early, in order to give them a chance. Throughout the time I knew him, I sensed that Chris was a troubled soul who needed help and reassurance. At school he was very shy and could be a real loner, and that continued at Leicestershire, although there were times when he would open up and let me in and afterwards I would wonder why I had been worried about him.

What happens with a lot of athletes is that they blank out the thought of their careers ending or of injury putting them on the sidelines, so when the time comes that they have to call it a day they are not prepared. I was happy when it ended for me, but I had other options.

DAFFY

When Chris walked away from cricket at 32 I am fairly confident in saying that he didn't know what he was going to do with the rest of his life, although I am pretty sure he didn't wake up one morning and say to himself: "Right then, from today I am going to become a drug dealer."

CHAPTER 17
A RIGHT ROYAL HONOUR

So here I am, just an ordinary man who happened to be able to play cricket to a decent standard, as a result of which I got to meet the likes of Muhammad Ali and Elton John. Even now, I sit down and reflect on it and it seems completely surreal. Did it really happen to me?

Well yes, it did. And as good as that was, there was an even more special moment for me. There are people who claim that the Royal Family should be abolished. For me, the very idea is preposterous. The Royal Family do a wonderful job for this country and it is entirely because of them that a lot of tourists come to London. I am sure that some have this quaint image of bumping into Her Majesty in Regent Street.

We played a Test match against West Indies at Lord's in 1991 and the Queen was due to come and meet the team but, as was often the way of these things in England during the summer, we were rained off. I was bitterly disappointed, and I know that some of my teammates felt the same way.

But then we were told that we had been invited to go to Buckingham Palace to meet Her Majesty and I was incredibly excited about the prospect of not only perhaps getting the chance to exchange a few words with her, but also to see where she lived. It was a huge deal for me. Buckingham Palace is, after all, a place that the vast majority of people only get to see through the gates and on television when the Royal Family stands on the balcony after a wedding or a major state occasion.

And now here I was, somebody who had grown up in the capital, about to go through the gates. It doesn't work that way, of course – you go in through a back entrance. We were shown into a room and believe it or believe it not, we were served cucumber sandwiches. I couldn't believe it. Meeting the Queen over cups of tea and neatly-cut cucumber sandwiches!

Prince Philip and Her Majesty then entered the room. We had all been briefed about the standards of etiquette that were expected of us so when each player was approached we all remembered to bow and we remembered to address her as 'Ma'am'. Before I knew what was happening, I was happily engaged in conversation with the monarch.

She had obviously done this sort of thing thousands of times in the past but I don't mind admitting that I was in awe of her. She made everybody feel totally relaxed, she appeared interested in what we had to say and she had a knowledge of cricket, or at least she had been well briefed before meeting us.

I guess that I spent 10 minutes in a one-to-one conversation with her, during which I told her that I had been born in 1966 in Dominica. "The year I was born, you and the Duke of Edinburgh came to Dominica and gave it its independence," I said. "My Mum's midwife told her that you were visiting and suggested that she take her new-born son outside to watch you go by. Such was the impact it had on my mother that she decided to call me Phillip."

She had a way of making everybody feel at ease. As daft as this sounds, you end up forgetting that you are talking to the Queen. She was a lovely, lovely lady and I admire her enormously. Inevitably, somebody moved her gently away from me and it was at that moment that I realised what had just happened to me. I'd been talking to the Queen, just the two of us, with no interruptions. And I was stunned.

It was a special day in my life, the day the Queen stood and listened to my story. My only regret was that I don't have a picture of the moment, but we were not allowed to take photographs inside the palace.

I have been lucky enough to meet some other extraordinary people. I played golf with Sir Steve Redgrave, when he was competing he was a ruthless competitor who knew exactly what he wanted to achieve in his rowing career, but in the flesh he is a different man. I really enjoyed his company, and found it difficult to equate the man who stood in front of me with the fierce Olympic competitor and champion I knew him to be.

CHAPTER 18
END OF THE RAINBOW

Having rejected Alli Bacher's offer to play for his rebel team, I did eventually find myself heading off to play cricket for Boland in South Africa. At the end of 1993 I received an approach and was happy to play for a team that was being coached at the time by Bob Woolmer, who would later go on to coach South Africa with such distinction and success.

My view was that I had never been there and it had supposedly all changed so this was the perfect opportunity for me to travel there, play cricket and perhaps pass on to the young players some of the things I had picked up along the way. I arrived in Stellenbosch, where Boland were based.

The team included Claude Henderson and coloured players such as Henry Williams, Omar Henry and Roger Telemachus. I did not think too much about the black players, coloured players and white players, as I was just there to play cricket.

I stayed in Stellenbosch, and I was told that when my wife came over to join me that I should bring her along to a brie (barbecue) so that everybody could get to meet her. While I was on my own, I was treated really well, as an England international playing for Boland. They gave me a house in a big Afrikaans area, with a swimming pool and a maid who came in every day, and I was made to feel extremely welcome.

After a while, my wife Nicky and my daughter Alexandra came to stay with me. The way that people reacted left me shocked – I had never seen anything like it in my life. This was a country that was supposed to be in the midst of change and reform, where people from different ethnic backgrounds were meant to be learning to get along with one another. But they were mortified that my wife was white.

They hadn't considered for one minute that I would be married to a white woman, and the coloured guys couldn't believe it. It was as if I had committed some heinous crime against humanity.

"What's going on Phil?" they asked me.

"What do you mean?"

"Well that just doesn't happen man. Black guys don't marry white women."

It had never been an issue for Nicky and I, but suddenly it was a huge problem for all these cricketers I had been playing with. That was the moment when I knew that the South Africans still had a long road to travel before they could say that they had dismantled apartheid, and the thing was that the coloured guys were just as guilty of it in their own way as were the white population.

And what of the guys who had told me that I must bring Nicky to the brie? I never saw them socially again, not because of any conscious decision that I made, but because they stopped mixing with me. After Nicky's arrival, not once was I asked to any of their homes. The only exception was a guy called Wayne Trouter.

The oddest thing of all was that when it was just me and the other players, they still treated me well enough. But whenever Nicky was around, or if I brought up her name, they all clammed up. Nobody wanted to know.

There was one coloured player, Craig Marias, with whom I had become good friends and he was seeing a white girl. He told me that the relationship had caused him lots of problems. He lived in Cape Town, travelling each day to play cricket, and he suggested I move there too.

"People have a different outlook in Cape Town and are rather more broad-minded, so you well find that things are okay if you decide to live there instead," he said.

I had already made up my mind that it couldn't possibly be any worse. I had been living in an Afrikaans area near Stellenbosch and went to see Bob Woolmer and told him that I didn't feel safe where we were living. "I feel really uncomfortable going out for a walk with my wife and having people staring at us. It isn't right. I don't mind travelling in for training and matches," I told him. "And I think that I would quite like to live in Cape Town."

I had never before worried about my wife and daughter, but now I felt threatened. In truth, the way I felt I would have happily got on a plane and flown back to England, but I had a contract to fulfil.

Bob said that he understood my feelings and promised that he would help me to find an apartment, so a few days later I went with Craig to look round a few properties in an area called Seapoint, while Nicky and Alexandra were with Bob. Craig and I came out of an apartment to meet the others, and Bob had been buying ice cream for Alexandra. I bent down and picked up my daughter and the woman behind the ice cream counter gave me a look as if to say: "Why are you picking that child up?"

"It's fine," I said. "This is my daughter, and that is my wife." There was a look of hatred and contempt on her face that made me feel sick to the pit of my stomach.

We moved into an apartment in Seapoint, but it still didn't feel right, and eventually I said to Nicky: "I am really sorry, but I would feel much happier if you took Alexandra back to England." And that is what she did.

The time difference between England and South Africa is not bad, so I flew home a couple of times to be with them.

What annoyed me most of all was that I would go out with Craig for a meal or whatever and when people realised that I was Phil DeFreitas, the England cricketer, they treated me brilliantly. But when I had been with my wife – my white wife – they didn't want to know. And when they didn't know who I was, they treated me the same way Cape Town coloured people are treated, and I am here to tell you that it was horrendous. That people could treat fellow human beings in such a way was beyond my understanding. Coloured people were made to feel like something the whites had stepped in.

It opened my eyes to what was wrong with South Africa, even though they would have the rest of the world believe that they had put their house in order. Going there as an international cricketer I was, on the whole, treated really well

Once, I walked into a shop in Cape Town and two white women looked me up and down. It was obvious that they were worried, scared even, because they thought I might have come in to rob the place. I felt like a criminal, right up to the point where I opened my mouth. "Oh, you're English," one of them said. Suddenly they were looking at me in a very different light, even though the colour of my skin hadn't changed.

On one occasion we travelled to East London, near Port Elizabeth, late on Christmas Day to play a Boxing Day match and I ended up spending most of Christmas Day on my own because I refused to go out. A couple of players invited me to their homes, but I didn't feel comfortable so thanked them but said I would cook my own Christmas meal, and meet them later at the airport. It wasn't one of the better days of my life.

There was a more reverential approach to black men and women who played sport for South Africa, but that also left a bad taste in my mouth. Why would you treat a sportsman any differently to, say, a labourer? Part of the problem in South Africa lies with the fact that a large proportion of the Afrikaans population do not travel outside their own country – if they did, and witnessed what was happening abroad, they would surely become more liberal and more broad-minded about events in their homeland.

I remember having a conversation with Craig's girlfriend's best friend, a white Afrikaans girl, and I asked her if she would ever consider going out with a coloured man whom she found attractive. Without any hesitation, she replied: "Never! It would never happen. It is not meant to be. It is not right."

I exploded. "Excuse me, but we are talking about another human being here," I said. "You can't help who you fall in love with, and it should make no difference anyway." It is an attitude that eats away at me. I turned to Craig and said: "Get her out of my face Craig. Take her away before I say something I will regret." To me, it is no different to a white Englishman falling in love with a white Frenchwoman.

When my first season at Boland came to an end, I wasn't broken-hearted. I left some good friends behind, and I had visited some wonderful places and felt that South Africa did have the potential to be a great place to live, but I wanted to get back to my wife and daughter.

It may surprise you to discover that I later returned to Boland. I had very good friends there in Craig and Omar Henry, and I knew that things were gradually changing for the better. Not only that, but I felt that people like myself, as coloured international sportsmen, had a duty to go back and prove that it did not matter what colour our skin was. If you are good enough, you are good enough.

There were occasions when I was in South Africa where I would go for a meal and they didn't know I was a cricketer.

Wayne Trouter took me to his home and we discussed religion and racism, and he treated me as an equal. Mind you, it wasn't like that everywhere. When we travelled to places such as Bloemfontein or Johannesburg, I wouldn't leave the hotel because those were cities that took longer to embrace change than other parts of the country.

There was also one overriding factor that took me back – I'd played really well in my first season and when that happens, you always want to return and do it again.

By and large, I have been quite lucky in England. You might expect that I would have had a lot of problems because of the colour of my skin, but it hasn't really worked out that way. There was one match early in my career at Yorkshire where the crowd made monkey noises and threw bananas at me in the outfield. I know it sometimes happens at football matches and players get really upset, but I believe the Yorkshire fans were just having a bit of fun. You could argue that it was a tasteless way to behave but the real problem was that because I was so young, I didn't know how to react, and I ended up in tears.

Winston Benjamin, one of my Leicestershire teammates, changed places with me in the field and picked up one of the bananas, ate half of it, threw it back into the crowd and thanked them. It was the perfect way to deal with it.

Early on in my career I sometimes felt that I had to be twice as good as my white counterparts in order to be given a chance, but once I had proved myself, it was never a problem.

CHAPTER 19
NORMAL SERVICE RESUMED

After doing well against Pakistan in the summer of 1992 I was really looking forward to touring India at the start of the following year, but it was back to normal service – one Test against India in Mumbai in February 1993. But, for me, cricket took a back seat to something else that happened while we were in India. You will recall that the game allowed me to meet, among many others, Elton John and George Michael, and those were pretty special moments in my life, times that I will tell my children and my grandchildren about.

The tour of India was one that I was really looking forward to. It seemed that whenever they came to England, I was always 12th man, and I wanted the opportunity to bowl against their batsmen and see how I got on in the subcontinent, on wickets that were very different from the ones we had at home.

We were meant to play three Tests and everybody was up for it and excited about the prospect. But then fate took a hand. We had been playing in a warm-up match and I went back to the hotel to shower and change, but the bathroom floor was extremely slippery and as I stepped out the shower, I slipped and I felt my groin go.

The upshot was that I wasn't fit for any more of the warm-up games and also missed the first two Tests, but I came back for a three-day game and bowled well enough and was picked for the Mumbai Test when we were already 2-0 down.

We batted first and Graeme Hick scored a sublime 178 – unfortunately, he didn't receive a great deal of support and we were bowled out for 347. India then amassed 591 thanks mainly to VG Kambli's 224 over 10 hours, a truly monumental feat of batting in stifling heat. I had dropped him off John Emburey when he had only scored about 20 runs. He had hit the ball way up in the air, I chased back for it and thought that I was almost standing on the boundary rope so stayed where I was and missed the ball completely – when I turned round I realised that I was yards and yards away from the rope, so it had been a complete cock-up on my part.

We were dismissed for 229 as India won by an innings and 15 runs and took the series 3-0. I didn't get a single first-class on that tour, hardly scored a run, spent the majority of my time injured and regarded it as the worst tour of my life but for one thing...

One morning we were told that if we wanted to go and meet Mother Teresa then it could be arranged but we would have to be up very early the following day. There was no doubt in my mind that I wanted to see this wonderful humanitarian who had done so many wonderful things. So Robin Smith, Neil Fairbrother, Dave Roberts and myself were up with the lark and were taken to meet her.

She was 82 years old at the time, and meeting her was one of the most humbling experiences of my life. She had an amazing aura and a sense of inner calm. Mother Teresa was a tiny woman and, incredibly, she spoke English. She had been told that we were members of the England cricket team but the game meant nothing when it came to being in the company of this woman. It remains one of the highlights of my life. We also had our photographs taken with her and looked like we had just got out of bed, which of course we had.

I was so overawed that I can't remember what she said to me but she gave each of us a card on which were written the words 'Gold blesses you and looks after you', and I still have it.

When I came back from India and people asked about the tour, all that I could talk about was meeting Mother Teresa. I was brought up as a Catholic and every Sunday morning my mother used to wake me up and tell me it was time for church – I would go mental because all I wanted to do on a Sunday was stay in bed. But once I got up and dragged myself along, I always felt much better.

I believe there is a God and I respect all religions because the way I look at it is that we are all still praying to the same God. I would not say that I am deeply religious, but I accept that it is very important for a lot of people.

CHAPTER 20
FOLLOW THAT

So how do you follow a meeting with Mother Teresa? By playing against Australia at Old Trafford later the same year, taking two wickets and being dropped again, of course.

But that Old Trafford Test will always be remembered for one delivery, one bowler and one batsman. The Australians had arrived with this young spin bowler in their team who had been hyped up, despite only having played 11 Tests up to that point with a fairly modest return of 31 wickets. Nobody could live up to the billing he had been given, except that he did.

We picked two spinners, Peter Such and Phil Tufnell, while the Australians opted for three quickies and their new spinner. Graham Gooch won the toss and put the tourists in and it looked like a good decision when we bowled them out for 289 and then put on 71 for the first wicket before losing Mike Atherton to the bowling of Merv Hughes.

Mike Gatting was the next England batsman in. It was the second day of the Test and Allan Border, the Australia captain, threw the ball to his new spinner. His name was Shane Warne and his first delivery became the most talked-about ball possibly in the history of Test-match cricket.

The ball started to drift right and Gatts moved his left leg forward, a standard way of playing such a delivery on the basis that if he got far enough forward and the ball hit his bat or pad then he could not be given out. However, the ball pitched outside Gatting's bat and clipped his off-stump, dislodging the bails. Gatts was utterly bemused, as were we all – he stared at the pitch for what seemed like an eternity before trudging off to the pavilion. Now we accepted that perhaps we were in the presence of greatness. None of us had ever seen a spin bowler make a ball turn quite as much – and it was his first delivery on English soil.

Australia won the match, and the series, without breaking sweat and Warne finished with 34 wickets. As with the great West Indians, I considered myself fortunate indeed to have seen Warne in action and to have faced him during my career. You can only judge yourself and the standards you have reached by the quality of the players you bowl to and bat against, and I faced some of the best this wonderful game has seen.

I don't suppose any of us had the first idea when we saw him at Old Trafford just what he would go on to achieve, but we all knew that we in at the start of something a bit special.

There were times when I faced Warne and I hadn't the foggiest idea what he was going to do next, which way the ball was going to turn. He was a master, an absolute one-off and a genius. People had different theories about how he could be worked out – watch his hand, watch his wrist. I tried it all but I could never fathom the guy. He was just far too good for me. Besides, I played on instinct throughout my career so with him I tried to focus on the length he was bowling, but he usually bamboozled me.

Towards the end of my Test career I faced him in Adelaide on a day when I did get my eye in and that was the only occasion where I began to feel comfortable against him. He could bowl the googly, the flipper, the leg spinner, and he had drift. I was always more comfortable facing quick bowlers who could hurl the ball down at me at 90mph because at least I knew where the ball was going.

And if I got hit by a bouncer I would experience an odd combination of anger and relief – anger because it had hurt, but I could at least now harness that energy, and relief because I knew it was out the way.

One of the things that made Warne stand out was that he never bowled you any rubbish, and that is a rare gift. You could never relax. Curtly Ambrose and Glenn McGrath used to do the same thing, but at much greater pace. Patience is the key to bowling well and taking wickets, and these guys were masters of it and finished their careers with hundreds of wickets.

I was dropped for the rest of the 1993 series, and when I didn't make the winter party to tour West Indies it did occur to me that perhaps my days as an international cricketer might be over, but in the summer of 1994 I was recalled alongside Peter Such for the visit of New Zealand. It was the early days of Ray Illingworth's regime, and Darren Gough also made his Test debut along with Craig White and Steve Rhodes.

There were three Tests, at Trent Bridge, Lord's and Old Trafford, and things went our way before a ball had been bowled with the news that Danny Morrison, their main strike bowler, was out through injury. But the thing with New Zealand in those days was that they always had Martin Crowe, who was all but guaranteed to score lots of runs, and Dion Nash proved to be a more than able bowling replacement for Morrison.

I bowled and batted as well as I had ever done for England in that series. At Trent Bridge, we dismissed New Zealand for 251 and I took four for 94. We then scored 567 for eight declared, with Graham Gooch smashing a double century and myself finishing unbeaten on 51. Second time around we bowled them out for 226 and this time I claimed five for 71 as we won by an innings and 90 runs. I was convinced that I would be named man of the match, but it went to Goochie, and I was absolutely gutted. What else did I have to do?

I followed that with six more wickets at Lord's in a drawn Test and another six at Old Trafford, where I also scored 69 runs in our first innings, as that also ended in a draw and we won the series 1-0. I was named England's Man of the Series after taking 21 wickets and Nash was their Man of the Series for his 17 wickets. Crowe, by the way, amassed a very impressive 380 runs.

Maybe I really did belong after all, and maybe I could become the 'next Botham'.

It was a busy summer, with South Africa arriving for three more Tests, and I was still on fire. I missed out at Lord's, but took five wickets at Headingley and four at The Oval, as well as hitting a bright and breezy 37.

We finished off 1994 by heading back to Australia, where we were brought back down to earth again, but I continued to bowl as well as I had ever done, taking four at Brisbane, three at Melbourne, two at Adelaide and four at Perth. And in the match in Adelaide I also hit my Test-best score with the bat, a glorious knock of 88.

CHAPTER 21
DOCTOR'S ORDERS

I roomed with Phil Tufnell on England's 1994-95 tour of Australia, and it turned out to be a memorable experience but for all the wrong reasons. His girlfriend at the time was working for British Airways, it was a fairly new relationship, they were apart and he wanted to be with her. The result was that he wasn't a particularly happy bunny.

He missed her terribly, right from the off, and was constantly on the phone to her. He simply wasn't himself. We were preparing for the Ashes and he was awake all night, every night, on and off the phone. And because he wasn't sleeping, neither was I.

It got to the stage where I had to go to the management and tell them that I needed my own room because he was keeping me awake. Part of the reason they had put us together, however, was because they wanted me to keep an eye on him because they knew we were friends.

He was in such a bad way that I expressed the view that we needed to get a doctor to come and have a look at him. A doctor was called and went to see Phil along with Dave Roberts, our physio, and the next thing I knew was that Tuffers had been taken away somewhere. None of us had a clue where.

I went out for dinner with a few of my teammates, including Graham

Thorpe, and we discussed what had happened and agreed that none of us could quite believe it. We were then told that a replacement had been sent for – Min Patel. It was apparent that whatever was wrong with Tuffers was fairly serious, but still none of us knew exactly where he had been taken – we assumed he was in hospital.

It emerged, however, that he was in a mental institution of some kind. We were laughing as we were told, but it was only because we all thought it couldn't possibly be right. I had known this guy for years and although he definitely was a bit different, he wasn't insane.

As it turned out, Phil agreed. We finished our meal and then headed back to the hotel and Thorpe came back to my room, where we were going to sit down, relax and chat. I opened my room door and there was Tuffers sitting on his bed. He looked up at me and said: "That place ain't for me man, it's full of nutters."

He hadn't been signed in, which meant that he was free to leave whenever he wanted, and he removed himself at the first available opportunity. After that he was fine – well, as fine as he ever was. It seemed that it had all been down to stress and tension, and the anxiety of being separated from somebody he had wanted to be with.

I first played with him at England Under-19 level and what people don't realise is that he could actually bat, but he was always scared of being hit by the ball. If he had ever been able to remove that fear then he could have been a genuine allrounder.

During the 1994-95 tour, we won at Adelaide, where I made my career-best score with the bat (88) and were 2-1 down in the series so went into the final Test in Perth needing a win to square things. I got my first ever pair in any form of cricket in Perth, and I honestly couldn't believe it.

It looked like we were going to lose the match and the series. I was in the changing room, and was watching TV as Tuffers went out to bat. There were a few other England players with me and we were all gutted because we'd had the chance of winning the game and had thrown it away.

Joe Angel bowled Tufnell a bouncer and he played it brilliantly, pulling the bat back and making no contact with the ball whatsoever. The Aussies appealed, and with that Tuffers started walking back to the pavilion, shaking his head, but the point was that he wasn't out – and he knew he wasn't out. But he just didn't fancy facing too many 90mph deliveries.

Having watched the replays, we all ended up sticking our heads in our lockers and fell about laughing. We were wetting ourselves, and then Graham Gooch came in and we knew that we had to suppress our laughter because here we were, just about to lose a Test match, and we knew that he wouldn't see the funny side of it. Eventually Tufnell came stumbling in, by which time some of the boys were actually in tears with laughter.

I tell you what though – with the ball in his hand, he was a wonderful bowler. He was a tremendous character and sometimes you had to make allowances for that, but he was always likely to pinch you a wicket at a crucial moment. Tuffers needed to be left to perform, and he would give everything for you.

At the end of a tour of New Zealand, I found myself sitting next to Tufnell on the flight home to England. I must have dozed off for a while and when I woke up I realised that the seat next to me was empty. Initially, I figured that he was in the toilet, but as the time ticked by and he still hadn't returned to his seat I started to look for him, convinced he had gone to the loo and had fallen asleep.

There was nobody in the toilet – in fact, all the toilets on the plane were empty. Starting to panic, I searched the entire plane and could find no sign of him. By this point, I was starting to get worried.

If you have ever been on a long-haul flight, you will know that there is an area, tucked away from the passengers, where the air crew can go and sleep for a few hours. And that is where we finally found Tuffers – sound asleep in one of the stewardess's beds. On his own, I might add, and oblivious of the panic he had caused. Ah yes, there was never a dull moment.

CHAPTER 22
MAKING IT COUNT

The team was experiencing mixed fortunes in terms of results, but I was happy with my form, and I was especially satisfied with my batting. I was beginning to make proper contributions on a fairly consistent basis.

Around this time a lot of people started to express the view that I had lost my 'nip', that I was maybe a yard slower than I had been. I had been playing non-stop cricket for a long time – whenever I was dropped by England I would be straight back to my county and into a championship match or a Sunday League game.

I was bowling long spells, over after over, often on wickets that were a batsman's dream, and it was tiring. It meant that I never came into a match feeling fresh. Under those circumstances, you cannot give 100% on every ball. I needed a break because I was aware that I wasn't bowling quite as quickly as I had been, but I also knew that it was because I wasn't fresh. The thing is that it was an absolute no-no to go to your county in the middle of a season and tell them you were knackered and needed a rest.

I remember one occasion when Mike Atherton was England captain and we had all played a lot of cricket and all got together and agreed that we needed a week away from the game – for me, that still meant training and practice sessions, but no competitive play, but that was a true one-off. We all felt the benefit of that though because when the next Test came around everybody felt fresh and raring to go.

During my career there were too many times when I was selected and arrived to play feeling way short of my best, physically and mentally – and Test cricket is not the place to try to hide away. You would finish playing a four-day game or a one-day game and then you would be straight into the Test arena.

The guys today complain about playing too much but I reckon they are looked after pretty well and get more chance to rest and recuperate than we ever did. It means bowlers can give their all in a five-day match and know that at the end of it they don't have to go back to their county; instead they will get some time off.

I hear commentators talking about how overworked the players are and it makes me smile because we really did have no respite whatsoever. I remember Neil Fairbrother and I played a one-day international for England at The Oval and when we were finished we had to get into our cars and drive straight to Colwyn Bay so that we could turn out for Lancashire the following day, something we did without complaint because it was just what was expected at the time.

The two of us were so tired that I suggested to Neil that we head to Manchester so that we could at least sleep in our own beds, and then we could head off first thing the next day. That is what happened, and as we were back in the car the following morning I found myself praying that we would be put into bat so that I could have some time to recover. What happened? We were in the field and I had to open the bowling. That was one of the few times when the love I felt for cricket reached breaking point. I knew that if I didn't bowl well or it didn't look as if I was giving my all then people would say I wasn't trying for my county.

Particularly as a pace bowler, there are times when you do need a break. County cricket is hard, hard work. Some bowlers need to play a lot to maintain their rhythm, but there has to be a happy medium, and that is where central contracts have changed everything. It is noticeable that there are far fewer injuries among England's quick bowlers now than there were when they were heading back to their counties between Tests.

West Indies were in England in 1995 and I played against them at Headingley, where I took a couple more wickets and scored 23 in our first dig. I was aware that my bowling wasn't as sharp as it could have been, but I had no cause to panic, or so I thought. There was, somewhere within me, a belief that my international career might be coming to an end I suppose, and it turned out that the match at Leeds would be the last time I would represent my country in a Test match.

In a way, it was probably quite appropriate that the curtain came down for me against West Indies because I always felt that I bowled well against them, and maybe didn't quite get the rewards that my efforts deserved.

My purple patch with England was 1991-92 when I took all those wickets against West Indies, Sri Lanka and New Zealand, and it is no coincidence that I achieved that during a time when I was given a proper run in the side. I was relaxed, secure about my position and not looking over my shoulder all the time. To put it in perspective, I took 38 wickets in nine matches, and every time I had the ball in my hand I felt that I was going to get another.

"I can carry on doing this if they continue to show faith in me," I thought to myself. Unfortunately, I suffered a couple of injuries – now you would have thought that a player who had performed as well for his country as I had done, would go straight back into the side when he was fit; that is what I expected to happen, but things were never that straightforward with England. I was competing for a place in the team with the likes of Angus Fraser, Devon Malcolm, Chris Lewis, Paul Jarvis, and then there would be the ones who would appear to pop up from nowhere and be picked on the basis of one or two good county performances.

When it all began for me I thought that having been selected as a 20-year-old, the powers-that-be had identified me as somebody who would play for England for 14 or 15 years. What I didn't realise was that I was expected to take five or six wickets and score 40-odd runs every time I played. Well I am sorry, but nobody can do that.

Many things used to eat away at me, but being called a one-day player really got me where it hurt. Yes, I could play one-day cricket, but I was proud of the fact that I could adapt to both forms of the game, and my record proved that. The thing is that if you keep reading that sort of nonsense, eventually the doubts begin to creep in and you start to wonder if maybe everybody else is right and you are wrong.

I didn't officially retire from international cricket because I was never given the opportunity to do so. Eventually you realise that you are not going to be picked any more – in my case I could not understand why – so you stop thinking of yourself as an England cricketer and begin to focus all your attention on your county career, or what is left of it. It is pretty devastating to realise that you have been discarded and that nobody has had the decency to explain why.

I wasn't the only one who received shabby treatment by England – Graeme Hick was another, and so was Mark Ramprakash. Hick, in particular, was treated very poorly. There were huge expectations of his ability and they were unreasonable. He was a superb batsman, but he was portrayed as some sort of batting Messiah, the answer to all England's problems. The pressure on his shoulders must have been immense, and then, of course, the press turned on him and treated him with utter contempt when he failed to go out and score centuries at will. No human being should ever be subjected to that kind of treatment.

I came into the team at about the same time as Ramprakash, or Ramps as he is universally known. England had a golden opportunity to tell these two young cricketers just to go out and enjoy themselves, to score runs and take wickets and not worry about anything else. Instead, as I said earlier, we felt that failure was not an option, so we didn't play with freedom. When everything you do is being scrutinised, how could we?

Just look at what the likes of Ramps has achieved in county cricket, where coaches had faith in him. And the same applies to Hick. Both these batsmen should still have been playing for England well into their thirties and should have been able to choose the time to call it a day at Test level instead of being dumped on the scrap heap without really having been given a fair crack of the whip.

The crazy thing is that England was considering recalling Ramps when he was nearly 40 because of his incredible form in county cricket. I hear people saying that he is a better player now than he was when he played for England, but that is utter rubbish – he was always a great batsman, but he knew that at county level people were always going to show faith in him, and that he wouldn't be dropped after a couple of failures.

Graham Gooch and Steve Waugh both made dreadful starts to their Test careers. Thankfully, the England and Australia selectors stuck with them and they went on to become two of the best international batsmen the world has seen.

Steve Harmison did not become a bad bowler overnight. Yes, his first delivery in the 2006 series in Australia was a shocker, but it wasn't his fault that England lost that Ashes series 5-0. The entire side had to accept collective blame for that – not that you would ever have known it from the way Harmison was slaughtered by the media though. I read all that stuff and it brought back a lot of painful memories; once again, it seemed that we had to find a scapegoat for our performance, somebody that could be hung out to dry, and it was extremely unfair that Harmison was the player the press picked on.

Another one of my regrets is that despite touring Australia, Pakistan, New Zealand, West Indies and India with England, I never really got the opportunity to see those countries. We would do three things – play, train and travel. And when we had the odd free day most of us would do very little because we saw it as an opportunity to recover from the exertions of Test cricket. I went to Australia but didn't get to see Ayers Rock or visit the Sydney Opera House, and I played in India but didn't get to the Taj Mahal, even though I was given the opportunity to see it.

The most we would do was perhaps wander round the shops nearest to the hotel and then come back and chill out or, if we were feeling particularly energetic, we might fit in a round of golf. There was also an element of thinking that there would be plenty of other opportunities in the future to come back to these countries and then maybe you would do the tourist thing.

Rest days were important for all the players. When you spend five days playing cricket in somewhere like India or Pakistan, you don't have a great deal of energy left at the end of it all. I loved what I saw of India. There is a lot of poverty, and there is no escaping from it, but the people all seem incredibly happy, and nothing appears to get them down.

I also only have good memories of Pakistan, where I was treated well by players and fans alike. Of course it is a shame that the game in Pakistan seems to be riven with allegations of corruption, but I hope and believe it can be stamped out. Like India, the people love their cricket, and I am sure that they want to watch honest cricket.

Many cricketers retire when they realise that their Test careers are over, but I didn't even contemplate it. In some ways it might even have been a relief because it meant that I could concentrate totally on playing for my county, and that was no hardship for me. I set myself some targets, deciding that I wanted to take 1,000 wickets, score 10,000 runs and win some trophies.

I loved playing and I loved staying fit. Because of the improvements in fitness techniques now, players in all sorts of sports are playing longer than they would ever have done before. Graeme Hick would have carried on playing until he was 50 if his body had allowed him to do so. Ramps gets better with age.

There were regrets that the England door had closed for me, of course there were, but there was still much for me to achieve in the game. I carried on because I knew that I was still good enough.

CHAPTER 23
NO SECOND CHANCES

One of the great strengths of the current side is that players are given time to settle into the side. For reasons that I have never been able to fathom, I appeared to be a convenient scapegoat, but they should have had faith in me, stuck with me and kept me in the team. Why couldn't selectors show the same kind of faith in me that the Australians did in Steve Waugh? I am not saying that I was in the same class as Waugh as a batsman – we were very different types of cricketers. But who is to say what would have happened to Waugh had the Aussies decided to drop him early in his career? It might have destroyed his career.

As I watched Waugh develop, I found myself wishing that I had been brought up in a different system. If I had been, I believe my career would have been that much better, and I would have scored more runs and taken more wickets at the highest level.

At various times I found myself described as the 'next Ian Botham' - there is no such thing. Botham was a one-off, and it was unfair to put that kind of pressure on my shoulders. I wasn't the only one though. Every time somebody came along who could bowl and bat a bit they were compared with Beefy. I discussed it with Ian and he always said the same thing: "Don't worry about it, just be yourself Daffy."

At first it concerned me. There I was trying to live up to the reputation of the greatest allrounder cricket has ever seen, and inside I knew that nobody could emulate him. I had to make the most of the gifts that I had been given and prove to myself and to my colleagues that it was good enough to be the first Phil DeFreitas. I regarded myself as a bowler who could bat, but I was realistic enough to realise that I was very unlikely ever to be chosen for my batting. On my day, I could make big scores with the willow, but, over after over, day after day, I always knew that I could take wickets, and that is what I brought to every team I ever played for.

Many people thought that I should have taken my batting more seriously, but what England should have said to me was: "Right then Phil, we need you to bowl and take wickets, but we are also looking at you as a batsman and we are going to put you in at number seven, so you are going to have to score runs as well. You need to take your batting more seriously."

And there's the rub – I always looked at my batting as being a bit of fun, and when you are going in at eight, nine or ten there really isn't much chance of doing anything else because by that stage of an innings you are simply expected to swing the bat and see if you can score a few runs. The exception to that, of course, would be the times when you went out to the middle with your team in trouble and your one remaining recognised batsman at the other end – at times like those you had to think clearly, play sensibly and do everything you could to give him the strike.

I was always at my best when I went out and played positively but because of this fear of being dropped by England that was to haunt me throughout my career I was very seldom able to go out and play my natural game. The result of that is that you become tense, terrified of making a mistake and, of course, you give your wicket away.

There is not the slightest doubt in my mind that I could have scored 3,000 or 4,000 runs in Test cricket if only I had been encouraged to go out and play my shots. But it is all about being supported and being backed by the captain and by the management and selectors – during that memorable first Ashes tour I received that support, quite possibly because there were so many wonderful players in the team, but there was no real difference in my form between the winter of 1986-87 and the summer of 1987, and that was what hurt so much. I may even have been able to understand being discarded after a Test in which I had performed horribly and we had been thrashed, but that just wasn't the case.

We still had very much the same nucleus of players and I would have benefited from playing another full series alongside them.

What I do know is that being dropped 14 times by England during my career did absolutely nothing for my confidence. It is horrible because you get the sense that you are being singled out for blame and, in cricket, there is no way that one player can cost his team a result. Having had such an incredible start to my Test career, I eventually reached the point where I used to dread the announcement of the England side.

I am proud of the fact that when England dropped me in 1987 I did not let it affect me. Yes I was disappointed – very disappointed; and I could easily have let my head fall but I kept performing well for Leicestershire with bat and ball. I suppose that it made me all the more determined to improve and to get back into the Test side.

Over the years, my county record stands comparison with most, which is more than can be said for some of the England players who seemed to just go through the motions when they went back to play for their counties.

I lived and breathed to play cricket for England and for Leicestershire, but the difference was that when I went out to bat or bowl for my county, I knew that everybody wanted me to succeed, whereas I quickly reached the stage with England where I felt that I was always on trial and that they were waiting for me to fail – with that sort of mindset, you are always rather more likely to fail than to succeed, I'm afraid. I was always nervous, fearing that my next Test could easily be my last.

In such circumstances, you try too hard, your emotions take over and you are not being yourself. As a result, I don't think that I gave my best in Test cricket. I am sure that if you speak to Graeme Hick, he would tell you the same thing – here was a player who arrived on the scene with a huge weight of expectation on his shoulders, and if he had scored a couple of spectacular innings early in his Test career then he could well have gone on to become one of the greatest batsmen of them all; instead, he struggled initially and became bogged down by a fear of failure rather than an expectation of success.

I played 44 Test matches – it should have been more – but what I will say is that I deserved to play in those Tests because I kept proving that I was good enough to represent my country. I feel that I should have played 80-odd Tests, taken more than 300 wickets and scored 4,000 runs if I had been allowed to play the game the way I wanted and I had known that one bad game wouldn't mean I would be dropped for the next. Because I didn't get that support, the selectors will never know how good I might have been for my country.

People asked me if I underachieved and I always tell them that you have to look at both sides. If you are given the opportunity to do something in life with no strings attached, then the chances are that you will go on and achieve it. I wasn't given the opportunity so, no, I don't think that I underachieved, but England may have done as a result of the way they treated me.

A lot is said and written about mental toughness. When you are in and out of a team like a yo-yo, it is fair to say that you have to become pretty tough and resilient. The thing I found hardest to come to terms with, and still do after all these years, is that nobody ever told me why I was being dropped; I was never told to go away and work on my batting or my bowling or my economy rate. The team would be announced and I wouldn't be in it, and that was it. It was a pretty shabby way to treat an international cricketer, and I am sure it would not have been handled that way in somewhere like Australia. All it needed was somebody to pick up a phone.

On top of that, I didn't really have anybody that I could turn to for advice; instead, I just had to keep my head down and try to shrug of all the negative feelings that were bouncing around inside my head – I can tell you that sometimes that was easier said than done.

You will be aware that there is usually a party of 12, sometimes 13, players named for a Test, and there were times when I would turn up and know from the way people were practising that I wasn't going to get a game – in many ways that was even worse than not being named in the squad at all.

My perception was that the way it worked was that if you were an established member of the team, somebody like Lamb, Botham or Gower, then a number of failures would be tolerated, and that was absolutely the right way to do it. But if you were on the fringes, like myself or maybe Gladstone Small, you played one poor game and you knew you were not going to play in the next Test. It was a strange way to work and no way at all to motivate players.

I listened to too much advice and ended up working out on the weights and bulking myself up. While it made me stronger, it also meant that I lost some of my zip and flexibility. If you bulk somebody up it doesn't necessarily follow that they will bowl faster, as I learnt to my cost. It took me a long time to get over that. That sort of thing would never happen today because the backroom staff know exactly what will work for each player and, crucially, what will not work.

For me, the key to bowling quickly was to remain lean. If you are a bowler like David 'Syd' Lawrence, however, strength work was vital. It just goes to prove that you need to be sure the advice you are being given is the best for you.

Nobody knows their body better than the individual, and I knew that the path I had been advised to follow was not the right one for me. I always bowled at my best when I was really lean. It took me a long time to shed the excess muscle and become lean again but as soon as I did, I started bowling quickly and accurately again and rediscovered my best form.

All that I needed to do were light weights which helped to build up my strength without overdoing it.

Normally I kept my feelings to myself after being dropped but there was one occasion in 1993 when I gave vent to my emotions. Graham Gooch was England captain at the time and we were playing Essex at Old Trafford when I discovered they'd left me out again – Gooch, of course, played for Essex. As we took the field, I gave vent to my feelings as we passed the visitors' dressing room, screaming abuse and thumping the window with my fist – the glass shattered and landed all over former teammate Peter Such. Let's just say that I received a tasty fine and the glazier's bill for that little outburst.

CHAPTER 24
THE INTERLOPER

I had given my all for England and English cricket from the start. Every time I was picked for the team I felt myself bursting with pride, whether it be in Test cricket or one-day internationals – and that is despite being dropped on a regular basis and being made to feel like I was to blame for bad performances.

The article beneath was one of the most insulting it has ever been my misfortune to read. Henderson suggested that the likes of myself and Devon Malcolm were not 'unequivocal Englishmen'. It was a crude reference to the fact that we had both been born in the West Indies.

Henderson described British-born West Indians as being 'resentful and separatist, and said he saw no reason why Test players, including myself, should not share the same 'mentality'.

He wrote: 'At the very least, it is difficult to see how playing for England could be anything more than a means of personal enhancement and achievement for players of West Indian ancestry,' and he went on to describe us as 'interlopers' who had a detrimental effect on English-born players.

'The common experience of mixed groups makes it immensely difficult to accept that a changing room comprising say six Englishmen, two West Indians, two Southern Africans and a New Zealander is going to develop the same camaraderie as 11 unequivocal Englishmen,' he continued.

'All the England players whom I would describe as foreigners may well be trying at a conscious level, but is that desire to succeed instinctive, a matter of biology? There lies the heart of the matter,' he wrote.

They used a photo of me, and apart from questioning the commitment of myself and Devon Malcolm, he also named the likes of Robin Smith and Allan Lamb as others who might not be fully committed to the cause. Anybody who ever saw Smith or Lamb play for England will know how outrageous the suggestion was. These were men who cared deeply about playing for their adopted country. Of course they were still South Africans at heart but, if anything, I believe they would have tried even harder when facing the land of their birth.

It was poison, without any basis in truth. David Frith, editor of *Cricket Monthly*, attempted to defend the article, saying it was an attempt to start a serious debate.

He added: "I don't think it's outrageous ... If you have two countries in you then there are times when it must be a factor in your performance when you're caught between the two."

Frith may not have regarded it as outrageous, but both Dev and I did. I felt that the suggestion that I was not passionate about playing for England and that I didn't care was libellous. It was certainly deeply insulting, especially as it came from a man with extreme right-wing views who knew nothing about me, Devon Malcolm or any other black cricketer who had played for England.

Dev was treated very poorly by England. I don't know if they were influenced by what Henderson had written but in 1995, manager-coach

Ray Illingworth and aide Peter Lever took apart an action that had been delivering the ball at almost 100mph and also attacked his attitude. Illingworth even said that Devon had no cricketing brain – this was a bowler who the previous year had taken nine for 57 against South Africa at The Oval.

Anyway, after reading the article I was a pretty angry young man, I can tell you. "This just isn't right," I told anybody who was prepared to listen, and I was especially upset about the fact that out of all the players they had named, the big picture used to support the article was one of me. It was like they were telling the world that in their view Phil DeFreitas was the main one who didn't try to perform at his best for England.

Henderson didn't know me, and he had made no effort to speak to me before writing his article. His view may have changed if he had known that I didn't really start playing cricket until I came to this country, so I felt that I had a debt to repay. It is a good time to state unequivocally that I considered myself to be English back then and I still do. I never had any desire to play for West Indies. Why would I?

This is where my home is and, more important than that, it is where my heart is. Does anybody really imagine that if I didn't love representing England then I would have been prepared to accept being dropped so many times? Of course not.

I spoke with a few friends, who agreed that the magazine had overstepped the mark, so I made up my mind that I was going to take legal action against them, consulted my solicitor, Paul Hackney, and he told me he was certain that I had a solid case.

People were telling me that I would get some money out of it, but my response was: "I couldn't give a monkey's whether I get any money. I just want my name cleared. I am only interested in getting it put right."

Initially, Devon didn't seem to be too interested in pursuing *Wisden* through the courts. He contacted the Professional Cricketers' Association (the players' union). David Graveney, the general secretary at the time, spoke to the association's lawyers, who came to the conclusion that Dev should forget about what had been written because, in their opinion, nothing could be done about it. The opinion of the lawyers Dev spoke to was that legal action would be a waste of money and that, in any event, the article was not libellous.

Unhappy with the response from the body that was meant to look after the interest of cricketers, Dev contacted Gordon Taylor at the Professional Footballers Association, and his reaction was very different. He told Dev that he would make the PFA's own lawyer available to him, although in the end that wasn't necessary.

It seemed pointless for us to be pursuing separate claims, so I suggested that Devon and I get together, along with our legal teams. The next stage in the process was that we went to see a libel barrister who agreed that we had a winnable a case.

Paul Hackney wrote a detailed letter to Wisden stating that what Henderson had written was untrue and that it had seriously harmed my reputation. He informed them that I required compensation, an apology published in the magazine, an apology read out in the High Court and payment of my legal costs.

Wisden soon offered to settle out of court and made an offer, which I was advised was inadequate. I was determined to see things through and told Paul that I wanted the matter resolved in court. I was determined that they were not going to wriggle off the hook. I wanted my day in court, and I wanted my name to be cleared – it wasn't much to ask. So, Devon and I began legal proceedings in the High Court.

As the days went by I received more and more phone calls, from MCC members and the like, urging me to accept Wisden's offer. They thought I was over-reacting but then again, it wasn't their reputations that had been brought into question. I did not ever want to be in a position where I might meet an England supporter and have him or her wondering whether I gave less than my all when I represented the country, so I told everybody who called me that they were wasting their time and their breath.

I told them all the same thing: "Nobody writes that sort of thing about me and gets away with it. I want an apology, and I want it done properly. We are going to court. Period." At the back of my mind there was also a grim determination that I didn't want the same kind of thing happening to anybody else.

At around the same time, an England Test squad had been announced to tour South Africa for the first time since apartheid had supposedly come to an end. Devon was picked but guess what? Yours truly wasn't. In the end, I went to South Africa anyway, to play for Boland.

The next thing I knew was that the papers were full of a story reporting that Devon had instructed his solicitors to settle out of court. To this day, I don't know how much he received, and if he felt that was the best way for him to go then who am I to criticise him? But it did leave me on my own.

In the end, *Wisden* agreed to print a full retraction, make a statement of apology in the High Court, which was the subject of much media interest, and to pay me a decent sum of money. I put some of the money towards extending my house, and the rest of which went to charity. As I said, for me this had never been about the money, but it had been everything to do with the damage I believed had been done to my reputation.

I was very pleased with the apologies, and I guess Devon was happy with the way if worked out for him too. One of the things I want to make crystal clear here is that Devon and I were good mates and we still are.

CHAPTER 25
PUTTING THE FAMILY FIRST

Nicola and I decided that we needed a bigger house, so we moved to just outside Warrington, but before long Nicola began to feel isolated – she had made friends where we were before and now she had to start all over again, with me away from home for much of the time. Alexandra was asthmatic and that only heightened Nicola's sense of isolation. Who would she turn to if our daughter had an attack and I was away with England or my county?

I was conscious of what my wife was going through, so at the end of 1993, at about the same time I ended up going to play for Boland, I came to the conclusion that it would be best for all of us if I moved to another county. I was still young enough at 27 to be able to offer a great deal and I wanted to make life better for both my wife and daughter – if she was going to be ill, it was imperative that she could get to hospital quickly if necessary and that there was a support network on hand.

For once in my life I made a decision that had nothing to do with cricket.

"I am really struggling here Nicola," I told her. "When I go away and Alexandra is unwell, I know that there is nobody here for you to help you through it all, and I know it isn't fair on you. I think it is time we moved."

Her parents lived in Burton on Trent and the nearest county was Derbyshire so I approached them and asked whether they were interested in signing me. I spoke to Kim Barnett, the captain, and Mike Horton, the chairman, and they both said yes, so that was that. Decision made.

Leaving Lancashire was probably the hardest thing I have ever done, but I knew that for the sake of my family it was the right decision. David Hughes did everything he could to persuade me to stay. He was brilliant in fact, suggesting that I could move to Burton and carry on playing for Lancashire, but I convinced myself that it wouldn't work. I had to reduce the travel and the time I was away from home, not increase it.

Before I move on, there is something I need to say about David Hughes. During my time at Lancashire, some people used to say that we went out and played with only 10 men and that David was a passenger, but nobody who played for him would ever have agreed with that. He was a great captain and motivator and a thoroughly decent human being.

But, for me, at that point in my life and career, family came first and so, for the start of the 1994 season, I was a Derbyshire player.

I was fairly confident that moving to Burton on Trent would put everything right. It would mean that Nicola had a support network, that her parents could help her and that she could start mixing with her friends again.

What actually happened was that the two of us started to grow further and further apart. Nicola and I started to argue and bicker, and I began to dread coming home from matches because I found myself wondering what we would find to argue about this time. I hate arguments and any other form of confrontation because I deal with it by saying nothing, going back into that shell I have told you about.

It probably wasn't the best way to deal with things because by refusing to argue back or put over my side of the argument, it simply made Nicola even more angry and frustrated with me and I can look back and see that now. But the fact was that after everything I had seen, heard and been subjected to during my own childhood, I didn't want my daughter to have to go through the same thing – there was no way I wanted her to witness her Mum and Dad screaming and shouting at each other.

And then there was the time when I thought I might have lost Alexandra. Derbyshire were playing Essex at Chelmsford and the team were going out for a meal. Before we went out, I phoned Nicola and asked if everything was all right. "Yes, no problem, I am just going to run a bath for her." We had an old-fashioned tank that necessitated us having to put the hot water into the bath first, and then top it up with cold – you couldn't run both taps together. We had been thinking of changing it for some time.

So I said: "Okay then, I am just going out for a meal with the guys. Speak soon."

Alexandra, who was four years old at the time, was upstairs in the bathroom and decided to jump into the bath, which was full of scalding hot water. Nicola called an ambulance and Alexandra was taken to the burns unit at Birmingham Hospital. I got the message while we were eating, so I jumped straight into the car and drove all the way to Birmingham at a constant 90-100mph. I was numb, not knowing what to expect.

The next few days were horrendous, as Nicola and I sat by her bedside and prayed. Alexandra would fall asleep and then wake up after 10 or

15 minutes in tears. Seeing our daughter like that obviously reduced the two of us to tears too. Fortunately, she made a full recovery and did not need a skin graft, although she still has some scarring. She had to learn to walk all over again and there were some bad days, but Alexandra is a fighter and she battled through it all. Nicola blamed herself, but it was not her fault. Sometimes, things like that happen – it is nobody's fault.

It was Alexandra who turned round and said to me: "Daddy, you can go back to play cricket now. I am okay. I am better now."

We were both so relieved that our daughter had made such a good recovery, but the arguments between Nicola and I continued. I would walk away from it, anything to avoid facing it. And in the end, I walked away for good. There were too many things we saw differently. I was happiest when I was playing cricket, which meant there was stuff I didn't want to deal with – to be fair to Nicola, she was the one who looked after our finances because I couldn't, and I was happy for her to do that.

We gave it our best shot – in the end, we were together for about eight years. It really didn't help that I spent so much time away from home and when I would return it was only natural that she would want to unburden herself and tell me about all the little things that might have gone wrong while I had been away. Having returned from a tour of, say, the West Indies, the last thing I wanted to talk about was a broken washing machine or the fact that the car had failed its MOT.

I am delighted to say that Nicola moved on and found happiness with somebody else.

CHAPTER 26
PLAY AND YOU DIE

While I was at Derbyshire I received a letter from the National Front that went along the following lines: 'We are going to kill you if you play for England again. We are also going to kill your family. We know where you live.'

To say I was shocked would be something of an understatement. I showed the letter to the powers-that-be at Derbyshire and they immediately called in the police, who told me to ignore it. It was easy enough for them to say that – they weren't the ones with the threat hanging over their heads, I was.

But I took the advice I was given and decided to forget it and get on with my life, although I couldn't help but be worried about my family. Anyway, I would have been able to move on from it had it not been for the fact that a second hand-written letter arrived, and this one was even worse.

It said: 'If you step out and bowl a ball at Lord's, we will kill you and we will kill your family.'

Once again I showed it to my county bosses, the police were called in again and this time they took the whole thing far more seriously. Officers kept a discreet eye on my home in Burton on Trent, my movements were shadowed and we had to tape the letterbox – not only was this to prevent any more threatening letters being put through, but it made sure no letter bombs and anything of the sort could be delivered. It was a frightening time for me and for Nicola and Alexandra.

I also had to get rid of my sponsored car – there was no point keeping a low profile if I was driving around in a car that had my name plastered along both sides.

The whole thing was a real intrusion, but the worst thing of all was going to Lord's. I knew that I couldn't let these thugs win and that I had to defy them. If I had stepped down, it would have opened the door for them to do the same thing with hundreds of other sportsmen and women. And if that happened, where would it ever stop?

In saying all of that, as I approached Lord's, one thought kept going through my mind: "What happens if a sniper takes me out here?" That might sound melodramatic, but I didn't know what the National Front were capable of – I knew they certainly weren't people you wanted to invite round to your home for a cosy chat about Britain's immigration policy, that's for sure.

My view was that they were not going to stop me playing the game I loved. Nothing happened, of course – there were no snipers, and thankfully, there were no more letters. However, Frank Bruno received one and so did the swimmer Sharron Davies because she had dared to marry a black man, Derek Redmond. I remember watching Redmond taking part in the 400m at the Barcelona Olympics and he suffered a hamstring injury that left him in agony, but he was determined to get round and, helped by his father, he eventually crossed the finishing line to a standing ovation. It was one of the bravest things I have ever seen.

I struggle to get my head around the fact that the National Front consider themselves to be patriots when they are actually anything but, and I look back now and feel only pride that I stood up to them and refused to let them beat me.

CHAPTER 27
DERBYSHIRE DAYS

When Nicola and I split up, I had to find somewhere to live. One of my closest friends in the Derbyshire team was Paul Aldred. His father had died and his mother, Lynette, was living on her own, so Paul suggested that I go and have a word with her as she had a spare room and I guess she was looking for a bit of company. In the end, I spent the best part of two years living with Lynette.

I had some hamstring problems while I was at Derbyshire, really sharp pains, and I couldn't understand why. Trevor Smith, one of my teammates, had some hassle at the same time with shin splints, so we were both sent to see the club physio and I was referred to a specialist. It had been a cold early season and he told me that my hamstring wasn't torn, that I just needed to make sure that I warmed up properly and that I got some heat into my body.

Trevor, meanwhile, was in full rehab and was having to use crutches to aid his recovery. The pair of us were struggling to get fully fit so I went back to see the specialist and asked him if he thought the two of us would benefit from a week in the sun, maybe doing a bit of swimming and that kind of thing. He agreed, and I was delighted because I hated the idea of the rest of my teammates being fit while I was unable to play cricket.

I figured that if we went away, I could use the time to get myself 100% fit and start playing when I got back. So Trevor and I booked a place in Spain. We arrived in our hotel wearing tracksuits, and in the background we could hear music banging out, but we agreed that we would simply go for a bite to eat, have a drink and then have an early night.

Out we went, and we realised that there was a bar selling two-for-one drinks. Naturally we decided that we were going to have a bit of that, still wearing out tracksuits. About four hours later we were still there, both completely out of it. Trev was on crutches and I was still walking pretty gingerly, but we decided it was time to head back to the hotel, so off we went. Then I lost my footing and fell all the way down a steep bank.

"Daffy, Daffy. Are you all right?" asked Trev.

"Yeah, yeah, I'm fine," I reassured him. And I somehow managed to get to my feet and find my way to the room.

I woke up the next morning and looked at my tracksuit, which I was still wearing, and it was ripped to shreds. It was in such a bad state that I had to throw it away. Curiosity got the better of me so I went to have a look at where I had fallen, and there were cactus plants everywhere – how I had missed them, I will never know. Anyway, it turned out to be a wake-up call so we spent the rest of the week working hard on our fitness.

We had taken our break on the say-so of the club physio and an independent specialist, and hadn't thought anything of it, but when we returned to England there was hell to pay. The powers-that-be wanted to know where the hell we had been. Whoops! We hadn't officially cleared it with the county. Not a good plan.

But I was fit!

There was also a Derbyshire pre-season in Malaga when Kim Barnett was skipper, and he loved getting everybody up bright and early to go out for a run. One night Dominic Cork and I went out for a few drinks and then got back to the hotel and carried on drinking until we realised it was very, very late, so we headed for our rooms and set our alarms so that we would be up nice and early. We had been in bed for about an hour when the alarms went off and we got up, still drunk. Our plan was that if we were in the lobby waiting for Kim at 6am we would score a few extra brownie points because it would look like we hadn't been out at all and that we were really keen.

When Kim appeared, Dominic said: "I cannot believe we are the only ones here. What's the matter with the rest of them? Have they all been out on the booze and got themselves hammered?"

In the end we ran for miles on a hot morning, and the two of us were dead on our feet at the end of it.

Another part of the routine was that we would all get in a coach which would take us to our training ground and Kim would make the driver stop the bus at the bottom of a very steep hill, with still about two miles to go. "Right then lads, if anybody wants to join me in running up the hill to the training ground, get off the bus now," Kim would say. Corky and I would look at one another: "No chance." Meanwhile, the young players would reluctantly follow the skipper while we remained where we were. To be fair, we were always made to suffer afterwards though.

As it turned out, Corky replaced me in the England side, and I played a part in it. It was the second Test of the summer of 1995, England was already one down and both of us had been named in the squad. At that point, Dominic hadn't played any Test cricket.

In the county match before the Lord's game, he tore a muscle between his shoulder blades and Derbyshire were not keen on him joining up with the party, but it obviously meant a huge amount to him and when he asked me for advice I suggested that he get an injection and see if it did the trick.

The two of us travelled down to London in my car, which meant he was subjected to Bob Marley for most of the journey. We got to the team hotel on the Monday night and both headed for our rooms for a good night's sleep. The next day, heavy net sessions were organised and it was clear that David Lloyd, the coach, and Michael Atherton, the captain, wanted to put Dominic through his paces. I knew that wouldn't do his injury a great deal of good so I had a word with Bumble (Lloyd) and told him that Corky had bowled a lot of overs for Derbyshire so didn't need to do a lot in the nets.

Thankfully, Lloyd took my advice on board, and Cork was picked to play. Not so good was the fact that the man he replaced was me.

There was yet another pre-season, this one spent on Guernsey of all places, and it consisted of a week of very hard training. One night we all went out for a meal to a seafood restaurant. The older guys ordered sensible starters, but the young guys, trying to save a bit of money, decided they would have garlic bread, which was the cheapest option. Come the main course, the senior players had ordered various fish dishes, and the youngsters plumped for...pizza and chips.

When the bill came, we announced that we were going to split it equally. "But we only had garlic bread and pizza," said the youngsters. They were informed that we had gone out as a team and we would be paying for our food as a team.

The next day the coach addressed the young players. "Look at Devon and Phil," he said. "Look how smart they are, how well their clothes fit.

And look at the state of you lot. And I am not surprised, given that you go out at night and eat garlic bread and pizza." It was a priceless moment.

The irony was that all the players received a meal allowance but rather than spending it on something decent, many young players would buy fish and chips, just so that they could pocket a couple of pounds.

My first year on the playing side with Derbyshire was great fun. Barnett was captain, as he had been for a number of years, but at the end of the season he announced that he was standing down.

The next thing we heard was that Dean Jones, the great Australian batsman, had been signed by Mike Horton and was coming in to replace Kim as captain. Dean was a world-class batsman so everybody was delighted to have him leading the team.

Just in case you don't know much about Jones, there is a famous story that perfectly sums up the sort of character he was.

He was playing for Australia in only his third Test, against India in Chennai, or Madras as it was back in 1986. Anybody who has ever been to that part of the world will know how oppressively hot it can become. It was so bad on that occasion that Dean, suffering from dehydration, frequently vomited on the pitch, and told Allan Border, his captain, that he wanted to go off the field, 'retired ill'. Border told Jones that if he couldn't handle the conditions "then let's get a real Australian in" - he was referring to Greg Ritchie, the next man in to bat and, like Border, a Queenslander.

Jones' response was to tell Border he was staying out there and he went on to score 210 runs. Epic stuff.

Before the 1996 season began, I had suffered an elbow injury and needed an operation so I was out of action for the pre-season warm-up games. When I recovered I turned up at the ground and met Les Stillman, the new coach, and Jones, my new captain. Both men were Aussies – Stillman had played cricket and Aussie Rules football. They decided that they were going to appoint me vice-captain. I was chuffed, and considered it a real honour.

It meant that if Jones ever missed a match, I would be leading the side. I also figured that if they had appointed me vice-captain then it also meant they rated me as a player.

Dean was an in-your-face, brash Australian and I thought he was brilliant. He was the type of character who would have a real go at you if he thought you weren't pulling your weight or you had done something wrong, and he would allow you to have a go back at him. The next day it was as if nothing had been said – you started with a clean slate. It is a way of working that most people like. Get it off your chest and then move on.

He was a hard man to please on the cricket field because, like so many other great sportsmen, he expected others to perform to his own high standards. But I loved playing for and with him. I thought he was a brilliant captain.

When he first came to Derbyshire he would play the Australian way, with four slips, two gulleys. I told him: "You can't do that in county cricket Dean. Sometimes you need to be a little bit more patient."

"Nah mate, you're wrong. We are going to do it my way."

"But it won't work."

He started to listen, and realised that I was right, and the two of us got a good working relationship going. Once he got the gist of what his bowlers were all about, what they could and what they could not do, the angles at which they delivered the ball, he would set the perfect fields.

Notwithstanding my amazing time at Lancashire, that season was the best in the county championship that I have ever had. Without a shadow of a doubt, we should have won the championship that year. We lost one game to Leicestershire which we gave away when Deano insisted on setting them a target and they reached it. A draw would have given us the title. For a little, unfashionable county like Derbyshire, it would have been a truly amazing achievement.

The season came to an end and I was desperately sad. It was like my first tour with England, when we beat Australia Down Under. Normally, when you reach the end of a campaign you are ready to put your feet up and enjoy a bit of a break from the game, but I'd had so much fun under Dean's captaincy that I just wanted it to go on and on, and I am certain most of my teammates felt exactly the same way.

Training had been hard, but tremendously well organised. Suddenly, everything about Derbyshire was being run in a thoroughly professional way. But September came and Dean headed back to Australia and the other players all went their own separate ways. I wanted to bring them all back and just carry on playing.

Throughout the winter, I looked forward to getting started with Derbyshire, but Dean came back for the 1997 season and it just wasn't the same. Suddenly there were personality clashes within the team and there was friction where there had been none before.

Dean and Kim Barnett didn't get on. I suppose it must have been hard for Kim, who had been captain of Derbyshire for so long, so stand back and watch this brash Australian come in, shake up the club and the team and nearly win the championship.

All this infighting was going on and I could scarcely believe what I was witnessing. How could everything have turned sour so quickly?

A meeting was called. It involved Dean, myself, Les Stillman, Kim Barnett and the chairman, Mike Horton.

Dean stood up and announced that he'd had enough and he was leaving. I was stunned. "Come on Deano, you can't do that. The lads all want you here," I said. But he wasn't listening and he stormed off. I was really angry, so I walked out too. This fantastic Australian cricketer had put his reputation on the line for Derbyshire and it could have gone horribly wrong for him; instead, he had transformed us from a bunch of also-rans into arguably the best four-day side in the land. They should have been extending his contract and doubling his pay, but there were factions who clearly wanted him out, and I couldn't believe it.

Later, I got a phone call from Horton. "Phil, we would like you to captain the side for the rest of the season," he said. I couldn't believe my ears but I agreed to do it because it was clear Dean wasn't coming back and I wanted to carry on the work that he had begun. My first problem was that Chris Adams, our best batsman, was so disgusted about Dean's departure that he wanted to follow him out of the county. I sat him down and pleaded with him to stick with the side for a season and to give me his best shot.

"At the end of the year, if you still feel the same way, you can head off," I said.

Chris was a star. He told me that he would stand beside me and do his best for Derbyshire, and that is precisely what happened. I decided that we needed to make some changes because there were some older players who were not pulling their weight and were not setting the right sort of example for the youngsters.

So we had a young, enthusiastic side and we were heading in the right direction, doing well and moving forward. We reached the quarter-finals of the NatWest, where we played Sussex, and we set them a target of more than 300 which they eventually chased down, but I was optimistic about the future.

Les Stillman was also shown the door because he had been brought in by Dean. He was an excellent coach with lots of good, forward-thinking ideas, and he was replaced by Andy Hayhurst, the second team coach.

Then there was a contracts meeting and I announced that I wanted no part in it because I didn't regard it as my team and as far as I was concerned, I wasn't officially the captain (I had only been asked to stand in). I told them: "Unless you appoint me captain I am not going to come into a meeting at which people's futures will be decided." On the morning of the meeting, I arrived at the ground and Stewart Edwards, the chief executive at the time, called me into his office and told me he needed me to be present.

"Why do you need me? Where's Andy Hayhurst?"

"Andy has got to go somewhere with the second team, so it is just me and you."

"Okay Stewart, I will go along with that, but only as long as you make it clear to the players that any decisions taken about their futures are nothing to do with me."

He agreed, but as soon as we got into the office he said that it was down to me to speak to the players who were being released. My first task was to tell one of the young cricketers he was no longer needed and he left that room thinking I had sacked him when I'd had nothing to do with it. I had no idea why he was being released. It was a shabby way to treat me and it was a shabby way to treat the youngsters. Remember, too, that I was the one who had been all for bringing in more young cricketers because it was what I thought was needed.

One of my teammates was Devon Malcolm, whom I had played with for England and it just so happened to be his benefit year, which is always a difficult time for a player because there is so much for him to arrange. Dev had been a great servant for Derbyshire and everybody associated with the club wanted his benefit year to go as well as possible.

I had players coming to me and telling me that they couldn't come to practice because they were attending this event for Dev or that event, but I didn't know anything about it, so I asked him to communicate with me throughout the season so that we could arrange practice sessions around him and the players could support him. His response was to accuse me of trying to wreck his benefit season. I had no intention of doing that. My aim was to do a captain's job of conducting proper training and practice sessions because everything was such a shambles at the time, and I couldn't have players wandering off when it suited them.

The incident that caused a rift concerned a golf day he had organised. Matthew Vandrau and Paul Aldred, who were both keen golfers, had been asked – both of them called me and asked if it was all right for them to play, but I told them it was the first I had heard of it. I then spoke to Dev and he insisted that he had left a message on my mobile and my home phone, but I received no such messages.

From that point, it was obvious that we needed to do something to clear the air, so I organised a meeting with the chairman of cricket and the chairman of the club, Dev and myself. The idea was to discuss how we could help his benefit year and work out a way of events happening with my knowledge.

Dev got the wrong end of the stick and we didn't really communicate properly for a few months.

Despite all the stuff that was going on off the field, I thought we were doing okay, but it seemed that not everybody agreed.

Kim Barnett called a meeting with a small group of senior players, at which Dominic Cork, Adrian Rollins, Krikken, Anne Brentnall, the physio, and Barnett himself were present.

Barnett proposed that Cork be appointed captain, Krikken vice-captain and John Smedley as chief executive. Apparently Barnett told the meeting I would be happy to play under Cork because I'd probably had enough of the hassle anyway. Regarding John Smedley, it is interesting to note that his father was a regular golf partner of...Kim Barnett.

Adrian Rollins, who is a close friend of mine, attended the meeting because he was the union representative for Derbyshire as part of the PCA (Professional Cricketers Association) and it would seem unjust if he were not present. Furthermore, he posed no serious threat to the likes of Barnett and Cork, because he was focussed on the entire squad.

The chief executive while all of this was happening was Stewart Edwards, who had joined not long before from Essex, where he had been treasurer. Unsurprisingly, Stewart resigned, citing the stress of the situation at Derbyshire.

Not a word had been said to me, but I didn't need to be Gypsy Rose Lee to work out what was going on. What they did to Dean Jones was wrong, and what they did to me was wrong, but that was the way the club was going.

"We are going to make Dominic Cork captain and Karl Krikken vice-captain," said the chairman.

"What? Well what on earth do you think I have been doing these past weeks? Don't I at least deserve a chance to take things forward from here?"

The decision had already been taken. I later heard that certain players had threatened to leave. I want to make it clear that I have nothing against Dominic, who was and still is a big mate of mine. He was a brilliant cricketer and teammate and I loved him, but if you are chairman you don't go around interviewing players for jobs that somebody else is doing without at least making that person aware of what is happening. Or rather, you shouldn't.

So Dominic did become captain of Derbyshire and I was happy to play under him, but the coach was a different matter. Colin Wells, who had been one of our senior players, was appointed and, to be frank, I didn't feel he was the right man for the job.

I explained my feelings to Dominic, telling him that I would have loved to play for him, but that it wasn't enough to keep me at Derbyshire. I did try for a while to work with Colin, but it was no use. If you don't respect somebody who is your boss, then he is going to have a problem and so are you. I suppose I felt that he could have done more to prevent what happened at the club.

By now, the chairman was Trevor Bowring and he came to my house for a chat and asked what could be done to sort things out but I told him things had gone way beyond that point. "The only way I can continue to play for Derbyshire is if you appoint a different coach," I said. "Otherwise, the only answer for everybody is for me to leave."

I had signed for Derbyshire in 1994 and remained with them for five years. There had been some good times, there had been some great times, but I hated the politics, the backstabbing and the infighting. I constantly found myself caught in the middle of it all when I just wanted to play cricket. It didn't seem to be too much to ask. Under Dean, we had finally turned a corner and looked like a professional outfit, but now it was like playing for a club side where the left hand didn't know what the right hand was doing.

I spoke to Leicestershire and they told me they would be delighted to have me back at Grace Road and so, in 2000, at the age of 34, I returned to where it had all begun and thought to myself: "What a wonderful way to finish my career, to go back where I started."

But I couldn't have been more wrong about that either.

CHAPTER 28
SLY FOXES

They always say you should never go back. And they are quite correct.

The Leicestershire that I had left all those years before was not the same one that I had now returned to. I was shocked at how different the place felt, but made up my mind to keep my head down, stay out of trouble and play.

Having left a club torn apart by internal politics, the last thing I wanted or needed was to be subjected to it all again, but I quickly realised that there was some stuff going on behind the scenes at Grace Road too.

People had personal agendas, and I hated it. We were there to play cricket and if certain individuals had things they wanted to achieve then it obviously meant they weren't fully concentrating on playing the game. If you don't concentrate you can't possibly play at your best – that much seems pretty obvious to me.

It seemed that people were trying to work things for themselves, and there was constant sniping and backbiting.

Vince Wells was captain, and he was a good captain and a lovely man whom I got on well with, but there was a small faction within the club who had their own personal agendas and tried to drag Vince in to help them achieve their goals. It seemed that almost every day I would walk into Grace Road and people would be whispering to one another, or conversations would stop when I entered a room. It wasn't an atmosphere that was conducive to engendering team spirit.

I was always an early bird and one day I walked in and there were four people having a private meeting in the changing room. That cannot be right, and it wasn't what I wanted to see. I was determined not to take sides, to look after number one, but it was very difficult. It got harder still when Vince stood down as captain and they asked me to succeed him.

It was tough. On the one hand, I saw it as a chance to get everybody singing from the same hymn sheet, but on the other, we didn't have the best of sides. Leicestershire had won the title not long before, but this team was not capable of achieving that kind of success.

Phil Whitticase was coach by then and he was a brilliant organiser. I had known him since he was a young man and I knew that he had many strengths, but it seemed to me that too many of our players didn't show him the respect he deserved, and it infuriated me.

All you need is for one or two senior players to make it obvious that they don't have time for the coach and it will quickly affect the whole team. That is what happened at Grace Road. It also had an impact on Phil. He was and is a very good coach, but he must have felt undermined by the behaviour of some of the players towards him.

He was not the sort of man who ever went looking for a fight or for confrontation and, to be honest, the best thing he could have done might well have been to have had a huge public showdown with one of the players who was making his life so difficult. I wish he had been stronger. It wasn't his fault, and I hated the people who didn't give him the chance to show what could have been achieved if only they had listened to him.

The guys who gave him a hard time know who they are. They stabbed

Phil in the back and they did the same thing to me – and they did it because they didn't have the guts to come and speak to us, face to face. In my opinion, you earn respect; it is certainly not something you can buy or demand from other people. These guys were not respected by Phil, they were not respected by me and I am sure they were not respected by the rest of their teammates either. Some people didn't like me because they knew they couldn't get round me.

All I wanted from them was that they went out and gave their best, whether batting, bowling or fielding, and that they supported their teammates. But a small minority were not even capable of doing that. I didn't care whether or not they were nice to me off the pitch; they could have done or said anything they wanted, just as long as I was convinced that when they played for Leicestershire they were giving it everything they had. And some couldn't do that. They should hang their heads in shame.

It's like when you watch a tennis player and suddenly realise that because he has been given the runaround that he has stopped trying. I couldn't live with myself if I ever did that in any part of my life.

You get paid to play cricket. If you give it 100%, that shows me you are made of the right stuff, and I will always defend you and I will respect you. The most infuriating thing about these people is that they would always talk a great game but when it came to the point where they had to stand up to be counted, they were always found wanting.

We played against Lancashire and Andrew Flintoff and Carl Hooper were smashing the ball around and I turned round to one of my bowlers and told him to warm up but he refused, saying: "No, no, no, they are going to hit me all over the ground."

I really don't want to name names because if I did I believe I would be coming down to their level. Besides, why should I give them a mention in my book, because they don't deserve it. End of story. Well, not quite, obviously.

As bad as it all was, there was one bright spot for me. At Leicestershire, each player is given an allowance towards his sponsor car, so I started looking round and eventually found my way to the Sturgess Motor Group, one of the biggest garages in Leicester and I walked in and sitting at one of the desks was a beautiful young woman, to whom I was immediately attracted. Her name was Katherine and I didn't know it at the time, but her father ran the company.

She would tell you that I kept looking at her, and I guess that is true. You hear about instant attraction and it had never happened to me before but that day I felt like I had been struck by a thunderbolt.

I was single at the time and about a month later I was in town with some friends and bumped into her again and said hello and had a brief conversation. For reasons which I can't fathom, I didn't ask her out. About three months later, I was out and saw her again and this time I did invite her out on a date. I was really nervous beforehand, but we went out for a meal together and hit it off straight away.

Before long, I had fallen in love with her and asked her to marry me. Thankfully, she accepted and I was absolutely thrilled. We got married in 2007, not long before our first son, Barnaby, was born. Later, we had a second son, Rafferty.

After my first marriage, I'd had doubts about settling down again, but life with Katherine, or Katie as she prefers to be called, has been great, and she is a wonderful wife and mother. She has supported me in everything I have done and encouraged me in my career.

I also achieved my career-best batting performance during my second stint with Leicestershire and, wouldn't you just know it, but Lancashire was our opponent. In the first innings I had scored 96 at the close of play and when we resumed the following day I just wanted to get to my ton as quickly as possible. Peter Martin was bowling and I went after an early delivery and got myself out. As you can imagine, I was not happy.

There are times where you have a bat in your hand and you see the ball as big as a football – you have to take advantage of those occasions because they don't come along too often. I was fortunate that when I went out to bat for a second time in that match, the magic was still there. According to the official statistics, I scored 123 not out, but I remember it as being 128.

Throughout my career, I always did well against my former counties – when I left Leicestershire, I managed to find my best form when I faced them, and that also applied when I left Lancashire and Derbyshire. Maybe you dig deeper because you feel that you have a point to prove. All the counties I played for meant something to me so when I played against them I wanted to produce the goods.

Lancashire was a great club for me and I loved the place and the players, so whenever I went back to Old Trafford it was never going to be difficult to motivate myself. I have always regarded myself as an adopted Lancastrian.

People often ask me how difficult it was to motivate myself to play county cricket, where you would often be performing in front of one man and his dog. If I had just played a Test match at a packed Lord's, Headingley or Old Trafford, then yes, it was hard. Having been perhaps cheered to the rafters for every wicket you had taken for England, suddenly you would be bowling your heart out again, take wickets and there would be next to no applause. Talk about coming back to earth with a bang.

I always found it easier if my county batted first because at least then I could spend a little while in the changing room, relaxing and getting a feel for the atmosphere again. Please don't get me wrong – I owe everything to county cricket and I assure you that after a session, or two at the most, I would be back in the swing of it, but I am pretty certain that every Test player of my generation would have struggled in the same way.

It was never a question of not trying, but if England had won you would be on an incredible high and then come crashing down, and if they had lost, well I am sure you can imagine how difficult it was to get yourself fired up to get going again.

When you play Test cricket, every ball matters, whereas at county level it was easier to get away with the occasional bad ball, but it was what we put our bodies through for the Test side that made the difference and unless anybody has been through that, they would never understand.

Bowling for my county, I found it possible to deliver five controlled overs without resorting to flat-out pace and I guess there were those who saw that as not trying. It was nonsense though.

In Test and county cricket there is a lot of sitting around, and everybody has their own way of passing the time waiting for their turn to go out and bat. Some of the guys will sit and read newspapers, do crossword puzzles, read books, watch TV, listen to the radio or sit on the balcony watching game. For me, it was always about music. Early on in my career I discovered the music of Bob Marley, and it had the perfect tempo to get me in the right mood to play. His music always calmed me down, and I would have my headphones on right up until the moment when I had to go out to bat.

There was also a sound system in the dressing room and if I was next in I might sometimes put Marley on that and tell my teammates I wanted to hear it before I went out. Other guys might demand absolute silence in the changing room before batting. You have to respect the wishes of your teammates and learn that what works for them might also work for you, but if it doesn't then you need to find your own trigger.

Some players had bizarre routines though, none more so than my former Derbyshire teammate Karl Krikken. They say wicketkeepers are an odd bunch, and he always used to gargle TCP before going out to play. Don't ask me why – I never did figure it out. But I tell you one thing, when you were out in the middle with him, you could smell him from the other end, and so could the opposition. Come to think of it, maybe that was why he did it – to put the opposition off. In his defence, he was a fine wicketkeeper, one of the best I played with.

Then there was Neil Fairbrother, one of the most naturally gifted batsmen I ever saw. He was a livewire, always moving about, finding it very difficult to sit down and relax, and before he batted he would get very nervous and would frequently be sick. But it would never affect his batting.

When he got himself settled, he would get himself in the zone and would be absolutely focused on what he was doing. I would go out to bat with him, and it was common practice to have a word with the other batsman, to find out what the wicket was doing and that kind of thing. Neil's eyes would be still, almost out on stalks, unblinking – the way Irish golfer Padraig Harrington looks when he is absolutely at the top of his game and you know that if a bomb went off, he wouldn't hear it. When Fairbrother had that look in his eyes, you knew all was well with the world.

Warren Hegg, the Lancashire keeper, was another who seemed to live on his nerves when he arrived at the crease to bat. He would be so nervous that he would struggle to get his words out and would often stutter and quiver, but once he had faced the first ball he would be fine. Throughout the years I found that I developed a great relationship with wicketkeepers and thoroughly enjoyed batting with them – these were the guys who were keeping to my bowling so there is a kind of empathy between you anyway. I always found that the best way to be with Warren was to have a laugh with him between overs, whereas Neil was rather more serious. Different horses for different courses. Like I said, it is all about finding out what works for you.

For me, I always felt more relaxed with the bat in my hand if I was able to have some fun with the guy at the other end, but I know that wouldn't work for a lot of players, especially mainstream batsmen. I always found tension to be a killer.

I remember playing for England against South Africa at The Oval and Darren Gough wandered out to the middle to join me and we had a quick chat and agreed that there was no point just trying to keep the bowlers out, so we decided to play a few shots, and every time we hit a boundary we would laugh. We thought it was brilliant fun and it probably also had the added bonus of upsetting the bowlers and making them less effective. The crowd soon picked up on our mood too, and quickly joined in. I scored 37 runs in no time and loved every second of it. When you lose that sense of fun, it is a whole different story.

Gough was a really bubbly Yorkshireman who always seemed to be up. Very little got him down, and he was always prepared to try different things, even if it cost him a few runs. When he first came into the England side he was like a breath of fresh air. When he bowled, he gave it everything and he had a tremendous sense of self-belief. I shared a room with him when we were away with England, and shared some great times, on and off the pitch – it was me who picked up the phone when his first child was born and we were in Australia.

CHAPTER 29
SHOWN THE DOOR

I have often sat down and asked myself whether I would still have gone back to Grace Road if I had known what lay ahead of me, and do you know what? I probably would have done, because it was where it all began for me, and I am realistic enough to know that I owe a great deal to Leicestershire. They were prepared to give me a chance. Yes, I still had to take it and prove that I was good enough, but who knows what might have happened if Leicestershire had not come calling?

Remarkably, training was never a grind for me. You might think that as I got older it would have become more difficult to motivate myself to put my body through it, but my training got better and better, and I always found myself looking forward to it and keeping up with the young guys.

I would turn up for pre-season and somebody would say: "Haven't you retired yet?" And that would simply inspire me to try even harder.

The last two years of my career were the worst, but that had absolutely nothing to do with the ageing process or an inability to reach the required levels of fitness.

I was still captain and we had just beaten Lancashire in the Twenty20 and were going well in the championship too and were still in the cup.

As far as I was concerned, we were flying. My old mate James Whittaker was chief executive and Neil Davidson was chairman and I was pretty certain they would be happy with the way things were going.

After beating Lancashire, we had to travel to Durham on a Sunday for a one-day game and I was on a high, but some senior players were not happy with me because when it came to championship games I refused to pick them – they were not giving me enough, so I felt justified in leaving them out. If I give them a couple of opportunities and they don't make the effort then they have no right to play.

We got to Durham and it was raining, so we ended up spending a lot of time in the changing room. It is always a tough time, and everybody has their own way of passing the time. Some guys play cards, some read books, others listen to music. After three or four hours the game was called off and James Whittaker said: "Can you pop into the office tomorrow morning please? I want to have a word with you."

"James, the game has been cancelled – can't we do it now?"

"No, no, no, let's do it tomorrow."

As I drove away from Durham my imagination was running riot and when I got home I said to Katie: "I don't know exactly what's happening but there's been a lot of talk going on and all I have done is to keep myself to myself. I know that certain players are not happy with team selection. I reckon one or two have stabbed me in the back and I just have a feeling that after tomorrow I am not going to be captain of Leicestershire any more."

I went to bed feeling gutted, and angry at James for not speaking to me at Durham. He was and remains a friend, and I would have felt a lot better having being told there and then, rather being left to drive all the way home and stew on it.

Anyway, I walked into his office the next day. James and Neil Davidson were both there and one of them said: "Phil we think it is time for a change."

"Why? We are doing all right, aren't we?"

"That may be true, but we think it's time to move forward."

Davidson then said: "We will issue a statement and if you want to go and finish your career somewhere else we are more than happy for you to do so."

"What?"

So it wasn't enough for them to strip me of the captaincy, but they also wanted me out of the place. I refused point blank, telling them I still had two years to run on my Leicestershire contract and I was going to see it out.

"And I don't want you to put out a statement either. I will do that myself. Let me do it tomorrow."

I was angry but I didn't want to rock the boat so I wrote something that effectively said I felt it was time I moved aside and let somebody else take over, adding that I felt I had taken the team as far as I could.

We reached the final of the Twenty20 Cup, but I was dropped. Leicestershire then went on to win the trophy, and I was not allowed to play any part in the celebration that followed. I was particularly upset about this because I had played in every game leading up to the quarter-finals. Not only was I not part of the celebration, but I wasn't even invited to the final, and I thought that was just plain vindictive. After the match, I phoned Charlie Dagnall, the Leicestershire bowler, to congratulate him and he said: "You should be here picking up this trophy Phil, nobody else. It is so, so wrong."

Was all this being done just because I had stood up for myself? And in similar circumstances, wouldn't anybody else have done the same thing?

What a way to treat somebody. Don't forget that it was Leicestershire who had offered me the contract in the first place. Even if I was going to be sent to Coventry, I was determined that I would play everything by the book to ensure that I was paid in full until the day that contract expired.

The season came to an end – and this time I wasn't sorry. But all too quickly, pre-season came around. By now H D Ackerman, of South Africa, had been brought in as Leicestershire captain, and I found myself being called into the office again. This time they offered to pay up part of my remaining year if I walked away there and then. It was almost as if they were trying to find the most humiliating way possible to end my career.

"Look, I have a year left on my contract and I am going to turn up for work every day. If you pick me, I will play and do my best. If you don't, I will still be here."

Incredibly, I was picked for the first team for a few championship games but then they decided that they were not going to pick me any more, but I was the model pro. I turned up for practice and I played with the second team. And when I wasn't doing all of that, I was playing golf – at least it meant I was able to get my handicap down.

Through it all I tried to maintain my dignity, even though I was seething inside, unable to believe the way I was being treated. And I still had no idea why. As far as I was concerned, my form was still good enough to justify my selection.

The end of the season arrived and, at the age of 39, having scored almost 11,000 first class runs and taken more than 1,200 wickets, it was all over. Normally there was an official end-of-season dinner at which everybody was expected to wear either dinner suit and black tie or their club suit. It was a big deal, at which players who were retiring would be honoured.

But in 2005, there was no dinner, just a drinks reception in the dining hall we used when we were playing matches. And how did they say goodbye to me? The chairman, Neil Davidson, stood up, presented me with a plaque on which there was a fox (the county emblem) and wished me good luck with my retirement. And that was it. Thank you and good night. You might not be surprised to discover that the plaque went straight into the bin. What an insult!

I vowed that for as long as Neil Davidson remained chairman of Leicestershire I would never again set foot in Grace Road, and he finally went in 2011. I don't believe that too many tears were shed over his departure. There were also one or two senior players I wanted to have nothing more to do with. It left me feeling sad, not that I had retired, but at the manner of it. Nobody wants to leave like that.

One of the worst things of all was that I wasn't allowed a match that I could have called my last game, where perhaps I or the county could have announced that it was going to be my final appearance. After all the years of service I gave them, I don't believe that was too much to ask.

Instead, my playing career ended in match for the Professional Cricketers' Association against a Pakistan club side in a minor Twenty20 competition at Grace Road. It wasn't quite the ending I had in mind, but at least it was something.

While I was at Leicestershire I also had my benefit year, in 2004, and that was also a disaster. Let me explain what a benefit year is all about. County cricketers are traditionally not terribly well paid so as a reward for loyal service to a county, you are allowed to arrange a variety of events designed to raise money to help you when you retire. These include dinners, raffles, dances, golf days and that kind of thing. People also donate things, such as a venue to hold a benefit dinner, or a table at a social event that you can sell or raffle off. Compared with the amounts of money some footballers are able to raise, it is a drop in the ocean, but it can be a life-saver.

The key is that everything is donated – if it was given to you, then you would have to pay tax on it. Clear as mud? Good.

Throughout my benefit year I had no support from Leicestershire. This was a real problem because as an active player, there is only so much you can do yourself. Some counties are brilliant when it comes to benefits and will take everything away from the player and organise the lot. I had no such luck.

Normally you would get the gate money from a couple of specified games, and you are also allowed to organise a collection, and I told the club that I would very much like the collections to be done at two Twenty20 matches, but was told that was out of the question because those games were specifically for the club.

The games where I was given permission to have collections were Mickey Mouse matches attended by one man and his dog.

I had moved around but I hadn't been given a benefit year anywhere else, and it somehow seemed right that I should have it at Leicestershire, where I started and finished my career. It ought to have been perfect, but it wasn't and the lack of support disappointed me and meant that I didn't raise as much as I might otherwise have done. Let's put it this way – the taxman has taken an interest in the money raised by some players, but they didn't trouble me.

On the upside, Sir Trevor McDonald helped me out with my benefit. I had met him at various cricket events, and realised he loved the sport with a passion. Over the years, the two of us have become friends and he flew up to Manchester for an Ashes reunion. We just hit it off, and I have nothing but respect for him. The likes of Phil Tufnell, Martin Johnson and Tim Brooke-Taylor also played a big part in my benefit year.

Those last two years were mental torture for me. In other circumstances, I might have dreaded giving up something that had dominated so much of my life but in the end it was a relief to retire, walk away and think about starting the next phase of my life. I knew that things could only get better. And this time I was right.

CHAPTER 30
GIVING SOMETHING BACK

After leaving Leicestershire, I wasn't quite ready to hang up my boots just yet so when I was offered the chance to join Hong Kong Cricket Club I jumped at it. I knew that the next stage for me was to go into coaching, but first I wanted to relax a bit and get county cricket out of my system.

I needed to be myself, have a bit of a break, and I was told that I could do some coaching in Hong Kong if I so wished. I had already started taking the relevant ECB courses and had gained some coaching badges. Deep down, I knew that I would be good at giving something back and that I would be able to help identify good young players and help to develop their talent and turn them into better players. Towards the end of my county career I had been doing a bit of work with some of the youngsters at Leicestershire and discovered that, as I had hoped, it was something I enjoyed.

Some former players are awful when it comes to passing on knowledge, identifying and rectifying faults in players, but I was lucky enough to discover that I seemed to have a natural talent for it.

Katie and I didn't have children at the time, so she came out to Hong Kong with me and we had a wonderful time together. We stayed there for six months and although I was asked to stay on, I felt that I had got everything out of my system and that it was the right time to return to England. Apart from anything else, Hong Kong was not the sort of place where I felt that I could settle – I would recommend that anybody go there for the experience, but what you have to realise is that millions of people live there and there is not an inch of spare land, so you always feel that you are hemmed in. It is claustrophobic.

When we returned to England, I was told by my agent that Nottinghamshire wondered if I would be interested in becoming their bowling coach. "Definitely," I replied. So it was that I did that for about three years on a part-time basis. For me, it was perfect way of staying in the game and continuing to make a contribution. I got to work with the likes of Ryan Sidebottom, Charlie Shreck, Darren Pattinson, Stuart Broad and Graham Swann.

After speaking to Ryan, it became obvious that he desperately wanted to play Test cricket for his country. He felt that he was good enough, and so did I. All that he lacked was the self-confidence, and being given the opportunity – in many ways, he reminded me of myself.

Ryan and I spent a lot of time talking and working on various things and I was chuffed to bits when he was called up and was not surprised that he did so well. I didn't know that he had been selected and I was walking into Trent Bridge one day and he was walking the other way and came up to me, gave me a big hug and said: "Thanks, mate." He didn't need to say any more. I knew immediately that he'd been given his chance, and he never looked back.

It was Ryan who did the work, it was Ryan who took the wickets and it is Ryan who deserves all the credit. I am just pleased that I was able to give him a few pointers.

I had passed my level 1 and 2 coaching badges while I was still playing the game (level 1 at Derbyshire, level 2 at Leicestershire). Then the England bowling coach's position became available and I applied for it, only to be told that I needed to reach at least level 3, so I went away on a residential course that featured three modules, one at Loughborough, the other two at Derbyshire, and then had to focus on lots of paperwork. Having attained that, the next and final step is to achieve level 4, but that involves a two-year course.

When I came back from Hong Kong in 2006 I was also approached by Michael Secreaton, who was chairman of Papplewick Cricket Club, asking me if I would be interested in coaching and playing for the club. It sounded like the perfect opportunity for me to carry on playing cricket and, most importantly, for me to continue to develop my coaching ability. I realised that I could do this in tandem with my work as bowling coach at Nottinghamshire, and it all sounded ideal.

Michael told me that I would have full control over choosing the first team, and that suited me down to the ground. As we were playing the first couple of pre-season games, it became clear that all the senior players were in the first team, while the youngsters – the future of the club – were turning out for the seconds and thirds.

My first job was to tell a few of the senior players that it was time for them to step down and allow the youngsters to take over. Naturally, it did not go down too well with a few of the guys, but I had been expecting that, and I knew that, for the sake of the future of the club, I was doing the right thing.

Early on, I identified a youngster called Luke Fletcher as somebody who could bat and bowl. He lived to play cricket and reminded me of the way I had been at the same age. I was thrilled that I had been presented with an opportunity to help Luke and to get him to believe that, with my help and support, he had what it took to become a professional cricketer.

Michael supported me all that way, and he also helped Luke in ways he didn't have to, such as providing him with all his kit.

So Luke had it all on a plate. Unfortunately, that wasn't the only thing he had on his plate. This was a lad who enjoyed eating junk food and like to go out for a drink the night before a match – how on earth do you go about persuading a teenager that he has to give that up, or at least cut down, if he is going to make the most of his talent.

I repeatedly told him how good a cricketer he was, and urged him not to let his talent go to waste. He should stop eating rubbish and join a gym with the money he would save by not going out at weekends. Every time I looked at him I could see his potential and I was determined that I wasn't going to stand back and watch him throw it all away.

It got to the stage where I was quite hard on him, on the field and off it, but he thought I was being unfair. I knew that some of the other players couldn't fathom why I was wasting my time on Luke, but I knew he had something.

Nottingham finally took an interest in him and got him to work as a gate-man in the mornings at Trent Bridge and in the afternoon he would train with the contracted players who had stayed at home in the winter. That summer, he played for Nottinghamshire second team was selected to play for England under-19s.

Luke was so excited of being picked for England that he decided he would not play for Papplewick on the Saturday – the England game was on the Sunday and they did not want him to play. I rang Andy Pick, who was in charge of the under-19 team and explained how nervous Luke was and suggested he played for Papplewick as a batsman but did not bowl. Andy agreed that it would help to take Luke's mind off things, but when I put it to the player, he was adamant that he did not want to play, and I respected his decision.

During the Papplewick game on the Saturday Luke turned up in his Notts tracksuit to watch his club play which I thought was fantastic. Then I noticed he was walking round the ground with a pint of lager – and I was told it was not his first. I had a word with him, telling him that it created the wrong image.

The following week I received a call from the Nottinghamshire second team coach, telling me that Luke felt I was picking on him. I asked for a meeting and Robin Rhodes, Papplewick's first team manager, with me and stressed that I only had Luke's best interests at heart and the last thing on my mind was to pick on him.

At the end of the season, I received a phone call from Mick Newell, the director of cricket at Nottinghamshire, telling me they were looking for a new bowling coach. He said the club felt they had enough experience at the club to take care of the first team and that the new bowling coach would only work with the youngsters, one of whom was Luke Fletcher, and since we had fallen out it would not be fair on Luke for me to be given the role.

This was a cricketer I had worked hard to help and support and I found it odd to hear that there was a problem between Luke and I because I had never seen it that way. Some time later, Nottinghamshire named Andy Pick, a former player, as bowling coach.

I now look at Luke playing regular first team cricket and with a big career ahead of him, and I feel proud that I helped in his development.

Naturally, I was disappointed not to have my contract renewed but then I was given the opportunity to start working with the boys at

Oakham School, which, once again, wasn't a full-time post but turned out to be incredibly rewarding. Next came a call from John Morris at Derbyshire, asking if I was interested in helping them out as a bowling coach. Because of the circumstances under which I left the club, I was delighted to be asked back and I suppose that I felt I had something of a point to prove.

I enjoyed it, too, but it was difficult to juggle alongside my schoolwork. Above all though, it meant a lot to me to know that I was wanted and that I was appreciated. In 2010, I concentrated solely on Oakham School, and set out to see how good a team we could produce. There were and are some very talented boys at the school, but I don't intend to put any extra pressure on their shoulders by singling out individuals.

And I didn't just teach cricket. In the winter, I also took charge of football, which I also loved. So here I was teaching my two favourite sports to a willing young audience. How good was that?

I enjoyed my time there enormously and will never forget the chance the school gave me. I have found out something about myself too, both as a person and as a coach. Sometimes, you need to handle boys with kid gloves, but there are also boys who respond better to a firmer approach, and getting the balance right is an art.

Throughout all of this, I played for Lashings, the club set up by David Folb and consisting of many of the best former Test players the world has ever seen. They may be getting on in years, but when the likes of Viv Richards goes out to the middle, he still wants to score as many runs as possible, and he hates getting out now as much as ever he did in his prime.

The Lashings matches are great fun, and I still really enjoy it because I keep myself fit, so I don't feel like I am struggling to keep up or to compete. Of course, there is no pressure on anybody's shoulders. We turn up for charity matches, have a bat, have a bowl, spend time on people's tables, answering their questions and telling them what Ian Botham is really like (don't worry Beefy, I only tell them what I think they want to hear!).

CHAPTER 31
PARALYSIS BY ANALYSIS

When I got home from Grace Road for the last time, Katie said that she saw an immediate difference in me – for the better, I might add. As relieved as I was, when it came to the first pre-season after I had retired, I was like a caged animal, a bear with a sore head. In many ways, pre-season was like Christmas all over again because that was when we would be given our new kit for the season, and when we would be reunited with guys we hadn't seen for weeks.

We would come back at the start of March, undergo fitness tests (I looked after myself so it was never a problem for me). Some guys put on weight over the winter so the first thing that happened with them was that they would be given extra work to do. I could never understand why they let themselves get into that state and I used to try to persuade them to knuckle down. "If you got yourself properly fit and ate the right diet, you would be amazed at just how much better you will play," I would say to them. Some people are prepared to cruise through their careers though and nothing any of us could say would make any difference.

Because I worked out during the winter, I did sometimes get upset when I saw men return for the season and it was obvious they had done nothing at all on the fitness front since the end of the previous campaign. Somehow, they got away with it, but those were the players whose careers were always up and down and they struggled to find any level of consistency.

The rest of us would focus on regular training, which gave me a buzz, and I don't mind admitting that I miss it still. I am a great believer in the saying that you get out of life what you put into it. During a training session I would be told that I had to bowl for half an hour, but at the end of it I would tell the coach I wanted to continue.

It was all about getting your technique and action right. Nobody is perfect and there were occasions when things didn't feel right, so I would first ask the wicketkeeper, who got a better view of my bowling action than anybody else, and then the coach if they could see anything that wasn't quite right. I would always receive lots of different answers and I would go away and think about them all and identify the one that made the most sense. Phil Whitticase, the keeper at Leicestershire, knew my game inside and out and he was usually the man who could help me. It is like golf coaches – the top pros stick with a teacher because they want to work with somebody who understands their golf swing, can take one look and immediately identify the fault that is causing the ball to go left or right.

There is lots of analysis available now, and players can go bowl and then watch their action on a computer screen, but I have always felt that a top bowler or batsman should have an idea of what it is that is going wrong without having to resort to that kind of thing. You know how you feel when you are playing really well, and that is what you attempt to emulate every time you pick up bat or ball.

It was a challenge to be ready and firing on all cylinders come the first game, and that was the thing I missed most when it was all over.

I had seen so many professional players become paralysed because they would have too many thoughts going through their heads. Cricket is, or should be, a natural game, played the way Kevin Pietersen does – you would never coach any youngster to bat like him; on the other hand, if you came across a youngster who batted that way and it worked for him, you would never suggest that he changed his technique. It should all be about natural feel, rhythm and timing.

Time and again I watch struggling batsmen take guard, and you soon realise all sorts of thoughts are going through their head apart from the one that should be foremost in their mind: watch the ball!

And here's another dilemma. A player books two or three sessions with a renowned coach and within a few seconds of the first session, the coach spots the problem. What does he do? He should, of course, tell the batsman or bowler immediately, and I can put my hand on my heart and say that I will always do that. But you can bet your bottom dollar that there will be some who will realise that if they do that then they will miss out on the fees for the subsequent sessions and will have the cricketer doing all sorts of other things until they eventually reveal the answer. And who knows how much more damage has been done by then?

I have always been wary about coaches who turn up with hundreds of cones because no matter what you do with a cone, or where you put it, you are never going to come up against one in a genuine match situation.

Coaching from a manual is not a good thing. It should be done by instinct.

There are also mixed views about the role of the sports psychologists. Some coaches swear by them and then, by association, his players will start to sing the praises of whichever mind guru is brought in.

At Leicestershire we had Ted Garrett, who would get together with the players at the beginning of the season and concentrate on stuff such as team building. There is a place for sports psychology individually, away from the rest of your teammates, but only if you are receptive to it in the first place. If somebody has a problem, they should feel able to work with the psychologist privately, without the rest of his teammates knowing all about it, away from everybody else.

My feeling was that pre-season was the wrong time because everybody has just come back and is already in a good, positive frame of mind. I don't believe it can work for a team – players will say what they think the gurus want to hear, but then the season gets going on all the back-stabbing will begin. What's the good of team building then?

CHAPTER 32
BIG BLACK CLOUDS

You have gathered by now that my cricket career was not always a bed of roses. There have been times when I have been treated very badly, both at county and international level, without ever being able to work out why.

When you put that together with the fact that I had a difficult childhood, both at home and at school, you may not be surprised to learn that there have been moments throughout my life when I have struggled to see the bright side of things.

The first time I was really aware of being stuck in a fog was when I was at Derbyshire and my first marriage had come to an end. I have always sunk pretty low when people around me whom I care about have not been fair and honest with me. Or when somebody has promised to do something and then doesn't do it. I feel let down and disappointed, and have this feeling of betrayal, and in those circumstances it has always been difficult for me to continue to function normally.

I was certainly able to empathise with Marcus Trescothick, the Somerset and former England batsman, when he revealed that he was fighting his own inner demons as he tried to get the better of depression. One of the problems with depression is that a lot of people will simply turn around and say: "Come on, shake yourself out of it. What have you got to be depressed about? You play the sport you love for a living, you have played for England and you have a good lifestyle. Millions of people would happily swap places with you."

It may be true that lots of people envy me and many of my fellow players, but there are no choices when it comes to depression. The most difficult thing is accepting that you have it, and then agreeing that you have to do something about it. Marcus was incredibly brave to admit how badly his depression had affected him. I am certain that he loved playing for England and that it was incredibly difficult for him to face up to the fact that he would have to end his Test career because he could not cope with being away from home.

With me, I have always felt a sense of injustice if somebody criticised me or said something that I considered to be hurtful, even if it wasn't meant to be. I also hate to have too much time on my hands because I sit and brood – my whole life has been about training, playing, training.

I was deeply affected by the outcome of games too. There was nobody better to be around when the team had won, especially if I felt that I had made a contribution with bat or ball. Equally, I used to stew on bad results, unless we had played well but the other side had played even better. There is nothing you can do about that. I especially hated losing if I thought that some of my teammates hadn't given 100%.

There was a big difference between the way I played county cricket and international cricket. With county cricket I would plan what I wanted to achieve, while with England I used to pray that it would all go right. I would prepare in the normal way and say: "Please, let me play well." In the end, I guess that put even greater pressure on my shoulders because I never felt able to relax and to just go out there and play my own game. I was so insecure. When I played for England I felt people were waiting for me to fail, but when I turned out for my county I knew that I had the support of my teammates and spectators and they expected me to perform well. If I failed to do so, they knew that I would make up for it the following day.

But even when I played well for England and took plenty of wickets in a Test or a one-day international, the insecurity never went away. I would feel that I had maybe secured myself one more match, but no more than that, and if I didn't do the business next time that would give the selectors the excuse they were looking for to discard me one more time.

There was also the added pressure that came from the views expressed in the commentary box by former players who really should know better. These are men who have represented their country and who know what it feels like when things go wrong. I have said before, and I repeat it now – nobody goes into a match planning to deliberately throw their wicket away or bowl horribly. Every batsman who has ever played the game has edged a ball that they know they should have left alone; every fielder has dropped a catch they know they should have pouched; and every bowler has had a spell where they have bowled like a drain. It is the nature of the beast.

What none of these guys want or need is for some ex-player – who may even be a former colleague – telling them how poorly they played, informing the viewing public that they threw the game away. It is almost as if the moment they give up the game, they forget what it feels like to be a player.

I know that when I was playing for England and I bowled a no-ball or whatever, I would walk back to my mark and I would sometimes imagine what was being said in the box, rather than concentrating on the next delivery. As with all the other stuff, it has a drip, drip, drip effect on your confidence and on your frame of mind. There was one commentator in particular, whose name I am not going to mention, who was ultra-critical of everything I ever did – I wouldn't have minded quite so much if this was a man who knew me and understood what it was that made me tick, but he made no effort to get to know me, finding it easier to have a go instead. It was horrible.

Geoff Boycott attracts a lot of negative press because of the way he is, but he cares passionately about English cricket and he would never say anything about you on TV or in the media that he wouldn't say to your face. I respect him enormously, and always have. After he had a go at me, I approached him and asked him what he was doing: "Phil, I am just being honest, and if you need help, I am here. All you have to do is ask."

I love the man, and he has been absolutely brilliant with me. Remember that he was one of the greatest batsmen who ever played for England, and if anybody is entitled to an opinion, then surely he is. You always know where you are with him. He is a typical Yorkshireman who tells you quite bluntly what he thinks, and he would never stab you in the back, unlike some others I could mention.

As far as my cricket upbringing was concerned, I was always told: "You do this or else." There were never any grey areas, and maybe that is why I have always got on so well with Geoff. What you see with him is what you get. You earn respect by being honest – I have always been honest with him and he has with me.

He loves being asked for help. If I had a flaw with my batting, I would have no hesitation in asking Geoff how I could correct it, and he was never short of an opinion. In the commentary box he would say stuff like: "Daffy has had a bad day out there, but he doesn't need me to tell him that. He will say so himself later on."

Raymond Illingworth was cut from the same cloth. He was another Yorkshireman who called a spade a spade but I will not hear a word against him because whenever I went to him and asked for help he was always there for me, and he never looked for anything in return, or went around telling everybody that he had set me straight.

Here's a radical thought for you media guys – when somebody is out there having a bad trot, how about trying to support him? You never know, the public may actually respect you for it.

And while we are it, let's get behind England. I found it more than a little bit disappointing that a poor World Cup campaign in 2011 overshadowed a fabulous Ashes victory in Australia in 2010-11. It would have been great to have won the World Cup, but as I described earlier in this book, there is nothing to top beating the Aussies on their own turf.

Cricketers are human beings. They are advised not to read the papers, but it is only natural that you want to read what is being written about you, especially if a friend phones you and says: "You should see what they are saying about you in the *Daily Planet*." Because I got so much negative press, it affected me throughout my career and it definitely contributed towards the depression I experienced. I was easily hurt by the things I heard and read. I wish that I could have been stronger, but I wasn't.

There is no doubt in my mind that my childhood deeply affected the way I turned out as an adult. I didn't enjoy it, and it is a source of constant regret to me that I missed out on Alexandra's childhood, first of all because I was away so much playing cricket and then because her mother and I got divorced. It meant I wasn't able to play my part in giving her the time she needed as she grew up; that is why I am so determined not to make the same mistake with my sons. I want to be there for them and do all I can to give them a childhood that they will look back on only with fond and happy memories. I don't want them to go through the same things I did, especially because I know that if they are unhappy now, it will follow them through their lives.

I consider myself to be a hands-on Dad, changing nappies, bathing them, taking them swimming and all that kind of stuff.

So you reach a certain age and you give up the sport, but how do you replace it? As a sportsman, one of things that gives you the biggest buzz is that feeling of adrenalin pumping through your body when you are on top of your game, and it is one of the things that is most difficult to replace when you give up. When I stopped playing, I discovered that going back to the gym and working out helped me enormously. There would be times when I would wake up in the morning and I would be in a mood, but I wouldn't know why, so I would head off to the gym for a session and it would always leave me feeling much better.

Although I am aware that it is an ongoing problem in my life, I haven't yet spoken to anybody about it, but I know that I should, and I will get around to addressing it.

A lot of ex-sportsmen suffer from depression when they retire, and it is hardly surprising. If you have been a footballer used to playing in front of 40,000 people every week with people chanting your name and suddenly all that is gone, then you would have to be a pretty tough character for it not to have an impact on you.

Part of the problem, I am sure, is that most of us don't properly plan for our retirement. No matter what walk of life you are in, you know that the day is coming when it must all come to an end, but people tend to bury their heads in the sand. "Oh, I will be fine. I will deal with that when I have to."

I had no idea what I was going to do when I finally stopped playing, and that is the way I have lived my life, taking things as they come, moving on to the next thing. Latterly, people would ask me what I was going to do when the time came to stop playing, but I didn't want to know. I had no answers for them, there was no great plan. The future would take care of itself.

Despite all the hassle I endured off the pitch, when I was out there playing, whether it be bowling, batting or fielding, it was the most wonderful feeling ever, and I didn't want it to ever come to an end. Every time a new season began, I wanted it to be special, and I never wanted it to end.

But it did end, and when it did, I believe that I became a better person. As a professional cricketer, if you want to reach the top – and I did – then you have to be very single-minded, selfish even. I was guilty of doing things like telling people I would phone them back and then not doing so because I was focused on the next game. It was all about me, me, me.

The people around me now tell me that I appear to be more relaxed for more of the time, and I know it is true that when I am with people I can trust then I feel much happier and I am able to let my guard down and have some fun. I have always enjoyed a bit of banter with the right individuals but then somebody would walk into the changing room that I didn't feel comfortable around and I would clam up.

I know that I still haven't got the moods completely sorted out, but things are much better now than they were during my playing days. I switched on and off when it came to playing, and I did the same thing with people.

CHAPTER 33
RISING FROM THE ASHES

Kicking off my England career with victory in the Ashes in Australia was a dream come true, and in some ways it was all downhill from that point. But I had no sense that when we flew home in 1987 it would be 2005 before England would win the Ashes again and that it would take until 2010-11 before a team from these shores would go Down Under and replicate what we had achieved.

I was aware that we were losing lots of series – indeed I was on the losing side in 1989, 1990, 1993 and 1994-95 – but I had no idea that it had been 24 years. It hardly seems credible.

I found myself in the media spotlight when it began to look as if we were going to win the 2010-11 series because, as people never tired of reminding me, I was the last member of the 1986-87 team to retire.

I was really made aware of it in 2005, when I was still playing and England and Australia fought out that wonderful series on home soil that left us with so many great memories, including Andrew Flintoff with bat, ball and beer glass in hand. At that stage I was the only member of Gatting's Ashes winning team still playing.

"My word, has it really been that long since we last won?" I asked myself.

The great thing was that after losing to us, Australia resolved that it wouldn't happen again. They picked and stuck with young players, they established a national cricket academy and they employed recent Test greats to pass on their secrets.

Because they were able to turn out so many wonderful batsmen and bowlers, they were able to bring in new captains and it had no effect on the team – they still kept on winning. The Australians have always taken their sport very seriously and they hate to lose, so when they do suffer a few defeats, they go away and come up with a plan to ensure it will not happen again.

There are not many sides who go to Australia and win, and you can be sure that they will come through the current sticky period – no team can lose the likes of Glenn McGrath, Matthew Hayden, Shane Warne, Adam Gilchrist, Damien Martyn, Steve and Mark Waugh and Justin Langer and carry on as if nothing has changed.

I like what is happening now in English cricket. Suddenly, we have that production line, especially when it comes to bowlers – Stuart Broad, Tim Bresnan, Jimmy Anderson, Chris Tremlett, Graham Onions, Graham Swann and countless others chomping at the bit. We have a batting line-up that goes deeper than it ever has, so if one or two or even three of our top batsmen fail, there is no cause for panic because somebody will get the runs. All the bowlers are good enough with the bat to face the best bowlers in the world.

It is great for the game in this country but I also believe it is good for the game as a whole. If there is a strong England Test side it makes other nations try that little bit harder to get one over on us because they don't like losing to England – and that means that if we are still winning then it means we are continuing to raise our game.

Cricket, like all sports, goes in cycles and I make no apologies for saying that I hope Australia go 20 years without winning the Ashes.

The England one-day side is a different matter, but the selectors are still guilty of chopping and changing. Why don't they identify the 11, 12 or 13 players they believe are the best one-day cricketers we possess and stick with them? Accept that there might be a few failures along the way, but take the pressure off their shoulders by giving them a decent run in the side. If you look at countries who win the World Cup, they don't do so by accident – they do so with settled teams. It is not rocket science.

One of the things that has always bugged me is that whenever we have had a period when we have struggled, everybody says: "Oh, it's the system. The English system is all wrong. We play too much county cricket, we don't play enough county cricket. We play too many one-day matches, we don't play enough one-day matches. Let's look at the Australian system. They have got it absolutely right with the number of state games they play and their academies."

So do you think that the Australians will now be saying that their system is all wrong and that they should be looking to adopt the English system? Of course they won't. Is the system they have used for the past 20 years suddenly wrong? No way. They will know that they might have to go through a painful period of transition but that they will identify quality young batsmen and bowlers in the long run and Australia will once again be a force, but let's hope it doesn't happen too quickly!

And let's be clear about something else – England's success has nothing to do with what is happening in county cricket. There are two divisions, and the standard of play in the second division is not great. In saying that, I am a big fan of the county game and I hope that it will survive. But please, let's find a way round putting players through a four-day game, followed by a one-day game, followed by a Twenty20 game. It is too much cricket, and it gives the best county players no time to recover.

The other thing you have to bear in mind is that our international players are involved in next to no county cricket now – they spend their entire time with the England set-up, thanks to central contracts, going back to their counties only when they are struggling for a bit of form and need to play their way back in again.

The way we look after our Test players today and help them to prepare for matches has changed beyond all recognition. People are also getting opportunities at a younger age – Stuart Broad and Alastair Cook are classic examples of that.

Purists may still turn up their noses at Twenty20 cricket, but nobody can deny that it is entertaining and that it has created a different kind of cricketer – indeed, many of the shots played at Test level would never have been seen had it not been for the advent of 20-over cricket. I also believe we have to recognise that it has brought a younger audience to the game and, hopefully, encouraged a few of them to start playing, and I am all for anything that achieves that.

It is exciting and is great for the paying public, who really get involved. When it was first introduced I didn't think it would catch on, but then I started playing and realised it was fun. It has also revolutionised one-day cricket – without Twenty20, we would never have seen so many sides scoring the thick end of 400 runs in a one-day game. Spectators love to see huge hits, balls being thrashed out the ground, batsmen being clean-bowled while going for impossibly big shots. It has been great for the game.

At the end of the day, the true test of a cricketer is the five-day game, playing for his country but apart from the Ashes series and any series involving India at home, the big money is in Twenty20 cricket, because it can be played at night, which means busy fathers can get home from work and take their children along to see a great evening's entertainment, at the end of which there will always be a result.

Players are now practising to become Twenty20 players because they know that is where they can make some money, and where they can make a name for themselves. Who would ever have thought it?

CHAPTER 34
CLASS IS PERMANENT

Like most sports, cricket will jump up and bite you when you least expect it. I suppose I was lucky in that I was considered to be an allrounder, so if I happened to be struggling with the ball, I could usually make up for it with the bat.

But if you are a Test batsman and you suddenly find yourself going through a barren period, it can be hell. It doesn't take long before the press start to turn on you, and then the fans get on your back. Everybody has advice for you, from the batting coach to your teammates to the well-meaning man in the street. And then, as quickly as you lost your touch, it can reappear and you can't stop making runs again.

If you are lucky, you will have survived in the Test side and you become a hero again – until the next time. Alastair Cook went through a torrid period in 2010 when he couldn't score a run to save his life, the media were calling for his head and, just as he was about to be hung out to dry, the runs began to flow once more.

But every time he had failed, the so-called pundits would take his game apart and highlight where he was going wrong. It must have been soul-destroying for an opening batsman who had proved himself time and time again against the best teams in the world.

I believe he did try to change his technique, but that didn't work so in the end he went back to doing what he knew and it all clicked into place for him again.

The same thing happened with Stuart Broad, who could be one of the best fast bowlers England has ever produced. At the start of the summer of 2011, he was even dropped for a Test against Sri Lanka, but then he was recalled to face India and bowled brilliantly against them. With his confidence sky-high once again, he began to flourish with the bat too – perhaps he could become the next Ian Botham after all.

Both these players now know that the selectors have faith in them – Cook wasn't dropped, and Broad only missed one Test. Let's be clear about one thing though: the England Test side is now the best in the world, and it is easier to stand by struggling individuals if the team keeps winning.

If, on the other hand, you are losing, there is always a need to find a scapegoat or two, and that is when players come in and out, in and out, and nobody ever feels settled. It makes the public think that the selectors are being proactive.

What used to happen with me was that when another allrounder was doing well on the county circuit, I would pick up the newspapers and the cricket writers would be championing his cause; without coming out and saying it directly, they wanted me out of the side, to be replaced by the latest big thing. I accepted it as being the nature of the beast but I wasn't happy about it. Wouldn't it be wonderful, just once, to pick up a newspaper and read a piece by a cricket correspondent in which he made a case for standing by a player? Some hope. I guess they would say that it doesn't sell newspapers, but how would they know if they don't try?

My argument has always been that when I was selected for my country, whether it was at Test or one-day level, then I had been chosen because they thought I was good enough. For all that I was dropped like a yo-yo, there were 44 times when Test selectors and England captains believed I was the best candidate for the job.

There were a few times when I would almost come to dread the team being announced, and not for the reason you might think. While it was bad enough to be dropped, I had a few occasions in my life when I really didn't want to be chosen because we were on a bad trot and I felt that I was on a hiding to nothing and that if I didn't deliver then I would once again be the sacrificial lamb when the next squad was announced.

Let me try to explain this more clearly. I would be left out of a squad and then I would head back to play county cricket. As I have repeated more than once in this book, I loved playing cricket so I wouldn't sulk over not being selected. Instead, I would get my head down, get stuck in and find a bit of form.

As you take wickets and the runs begin to flow from the bat, so your confidence grows and you look forward to the next day, and the next game. But I always felt that in those circumstances maybe I needed another couple of county games to get right back to my best. Then it occurs to you that England have lost the Test for which you were dropped, and the squad for the next match is about to be announced. Deep down I always wanted to hear that I had been recalled but at the same time there was that feeling of dread: "If I get back in and don't take five or six wickets, they will dump me again."

Confidence is everything. For me, it was all about knowing that everybody was behind and wanted me in the team, whether it be England, Leicestershire, Lancashire or Derbyshire. If I felt that I had that support I would almost always go out and perform well. Too many times I simply didn't feel that way.

One of the other problems in my day as an England player was that the selectors kept changing too, and I never believed that was a good thing. I am pretty sure that now Andrew Strauss, the captain, and Andy Flower, the coach, have the final word when it comes to the current England squad, but it wasn't like that when I was playing.

The only time that I knew one of the selectors had gone in to bat for me was when Raymond Illingworth was chairman of selectors and what Raymond wanted, Raymond tended to get. He came to watch me play for Derbyshire, spoke to me afterwards and hinted that I was in his thoughts, and the next thing I knew was that I was back in the team. He had told me he was happy with the way I was playing, that I had the right attitude and that I should be in the Test team. He wasn't everybody's cup of tea but I like Illingworth because you always knew where you stood with him. If he had something to say about you, he would always say it to your face.

I had always responded to that sort of approach when learning the game.

CHAPTER 35
OUCH! THAT HURTS

I have been pretty lucky when it comes to injuries. Some cricketers, especially pace bowlers, seem to spend half their careers on the sidelines, nursing back injuries, pulled muscles, side strains, knee injuries or torn hamstrings.

Indeed, injury ended the career of Andrew Flintoff before he had fulfilled his potential and poor Simon Jones was never the same after injuring himself in the field playing for England against Australia.

I tore my right abductor muscle while playing for England, and it took a while for that to get better. Matters were not helped by the fact that I hated sitting around on the sidelines twiddling my thumbs when I could be out on the field playing cricket. I was bored and restless and I came back too quickly. I am not the first to do that and I will not be the last – look at what Tiger Woods did to his knee by returning to golf too soon in 2011. He would have been better to have taken an extra few months out, just to ensure that he was 100% again, rather than hacking his way round and then walking off the course after an embarrassingly bad nine holes.

My abductor injury kept me out for a couple of months which, in the grand scheme of things, was nothing at all but I suppose that I was worried England might find somebody to replace me while I was out of the game, and I couldn't let that happen.

But every time I tried to bowl I would set it off again, and it ended up creating a lot of problems for me with my groin. It began a weakness that plagued me throughout my career – if ever I was fatigued and carried on bowling, there was always a tendency for my groin to flare up again, so I had to do a lot of strength work.

It meant that I had to be extremely careful with my warm-up routine – and the rub was the fact that I couldn't risk bowling unless I was properly warmed up. Everybody bowls in a way that is specific to them and it puts different strains on different parts of the body. The exercise regime I had to follow to keep myself in shape was not a problem for me because I enjoyed working out in the gym.

Later in my career I discovered that I had some floating bone in my elbow and that had to be dealt with pretty quickly because it caused considerable pain and discomfort. It is a common injury for bowlers and tennis players, caused I guess by the speed with which we move our arms.

It reached the stage where every time I bowled or threw the ball I felt a sharp pain in my elbow. When you are getting through lots of overs, at six balls an over, you will appreciate that it was something I couldn't allow to go unchecked for long. But, just like the abductor injury, I found myself putting the operation off because I knew it would mean that I had to take time out for recovery.

Eventually it got so bad that I was unable to throw the ball from the field, and then I knew that I couldn't put off the treatment any longer. The bone was removed and once again I was out for a while and even now, I cannot quite straighten my right arm properly. It didn't affect my bowling action unduly when I was fit enough to play again but I was in considerable discomfort for rather longer than I thought would be the case.

When you consider how long I played at the highest level and what I put my body through on an almost daily basis, I am very fortunate to have got away so lightly. There are some former cricketers who find it almost impossible to get out of bed in the morning, but I am not one of them and got away with a long career and no after-effects, other than – and don't laugh – that I suffer from bunions, caused by the fact that when I walk I drag my right foot ever so slightly. It is something that runs in our family, with my Mum also being a sufferer and at some point I am going to have to face the music and have it operated on and removed. When I was playing, there were times when it got so painful that I had to hack a hole in the toe of my boot to ease the pressure.

I went through a lot of pairs of cricket boots, but a lot of bowlers have similarly suffered. As I would run in to bowl, I would feel the pain and know what was going on but when we came in for lunch or tea I would never dare take my boot off for fear that I wouldn't be able to get it back on. And then, at the end of the day, the relief when it came off was indescribable but it was never especially pleasant to realise that my foot was covered in blood and that during the course of the day I had peeled off umpteen layers of skin.

Bowling a cricket ball at top speed is not a natural action, and it is inevitable that you are going to suffer a bit of pain or discomfort, but it is the way you deal with it that really matters. And can you imagine the response I would have got from the likes of Beefy or Tuffers if I had complained at the end of the day about my bunion?

You find a way to get through the day, tape up your toe and then go out again the next day and do the same again. There were lots of little niggles throughout my career but I refused to submit to any of them. If you blank them out, the pain will disappear, but if you allow it to dominate your thoughts you won't perform well and you will end up feeling sorry for yourself. You worry about the pain afterwards, and there were some days when I struggled to walk.

It is often said that to put themselves through what they do, bowlers must be stupid – there may be some truth in that, but there was never a better feeling than working out a way to dismiss a particular batsman and have him walk straight into the trap you had laid for him.

So yes, I have been extremely fortunate with regard to my knees and my back, which is where I would have expected to suffer, and a bad toe isn't too much to complain about, is it?

No matter how bad it gets, it never prevents me from doing the things I want to do. I still run on the treadmill and keep myself fit – and I am one of those rare individuals who actually looks forward to the gym.

CHAPTER 36
RECONCILIATION

My father and I kept our distance from one another throughout most of my adult life but in the end I had a choice to make. Did I want him to go to his grave without me ever making an effort to put things right, or did I want to try to re-establish some kind of relationship with him?

Despite everything, he and my mother have remained together, and I have always maintained contact with Mum.

The turning point came for me when I had my two sons. Up until that point, my parents had only had granddaughters. Now I am not saying that they would love girls any less, but I think that in any family there is always a special bond between grandparents and grandsons, if only because they ensure the family name lives on.

It was Katie who made the big difference. She has been brilliant and encouraged me to make an effort with Dad, if only for the sake of my boys in the first instance. When she told me that it would be totally unfair not to let my father get to know his grandchildren, I knew that she was right. And they had every right to meet him too.

After everything that had passed between us, it wasn't easy but he was in his seventies and you just never know what's around the corner for any of us. He had a health scare when he was diagnosed with diabetes and had to stop smoking and cut back on his drinking. The bottom line is that Dad has responded really well to the boys, who have perhaps given him something new to live for. He obviously loves them deeply, and they feel the same way about him. A grandparent can give a child something that their own mother and father never can, and there is nothing to beat a good relationship between grandparents and their grandchildren.

Prior to the boys coming along, I would go home to see Mum, and Dad and I would just ignore one another. I didn't want to make the effort, and both of us felt that we didn't want to be in the same room as each other, so one of us would always walk out.

As he has got to know the boys, the two of us have had to spend time in the same room and although we have not sat down together and had major clear-the-air talks, we have begun to chat to each other. It may not be what most people would regard as a proper father and son relationship, but it is good enough, and it is a whole lot better than it was and a big step forward. He still finds it difficult to let his guard down totally, and so do I.

I am sure that Mum is pleased that we are at least able to talk to each other now because she doesn't want any unpleasantness, and I can understand why.

There are feelings inside me towards him that will never go away, but it is enough for me that we have found a happy medium. Maybe in time we will be able to build something better but I reckon that where we are now is as far as we are going to get.

Sometimes he surprises me. He picks up the phone and calls me for a chat, but it is never a deep conversation, and it never lasts for long before he asks to speak to the boys. We've never gone down to the pub together or gone out for a bite to eat, and I don't believe that will ever happen. I envy men who have that sort of relationship with their fathers, and I am determined that I will be there as a friend and a Dad for my children. If I can do that, then I will have succeeded in life.

It is one of the big regrets of my life that Dad has never been able to tell me he is proud of what I achieved in cricket. I am sure that he is, but it would have been special to have heard it from his lips. Mum has told me that he keeps videos and that he talks about me when I am not there but he would never say it to my face.

He has always knocked me and has always been negative towards me. "You should have done this," or "You should have done it that way." It definitely had an impact on me as I went through my career, where I would allow negative thoughts to enter my head and would have to make a conscious effort to tell myself to stop it and focus on the positive things that were happening to me.

I don't drink much these days, but I do know that on the odd occasion when I have had too many, people always end up telling me that I am a funny drunk.

As to my future relationship with Dad, we can only carry on doing what we are doing and see where that takes us. In the meantime, it is important to me that Barnaby and Rafferty give him some joy and pleasure. They have certainly achieved that with Mum – when she talks to them I can hear the undiluted happiness in her voice. It makes Katie and I feel good.

Mum is a special woman – it takes a unique type of person to bring up seven boys, and she doesn't have a bad bone in her body, thinking only the best of people. Mum and Dad still live in Harlesden, near where I was brought up, and we go to see them as often as we can. Thankfully, they now have a house, with plenty of room. They still have the 50 acres of land in Dominica and I sometimes wonder why they don't move back there, but there is nothing there for them now.

As for my brothers, I try to keep in touch with them. Although I have moved all over England, they still live in London. We all get together if there is a family problem or a crisis.

Roland, Richie and Roy devoted a lot of their time to me and allowed and encouraged me to do what I wanted to do in cricket as I was growing up, and they were thrilled when England selected me. It would have been easy for them all to have moved away when they became 18, but they didn't; instead they remained at home to support their younger brothers. They sacrificed their lives for us and never got married. I will always owe them for that – they are special brothers who let opportunities pass them by just so that myself and my other brothers had the best possible chance in life.

It is expected when you write your memoirs that you single out the people who matter in your life. I have already mentioned the guys who helped me in my career, but when you make your living playing professional sport, you tend to make acquaintances rather than close friends. An exception to that would definitely be my former Lancashire and England teammate Neil Fairbrother, with whom I have remained in contact since we both stopped playing. Guys such as Chris Broad and Gladstone Small are also friends, as is Mike Gatting and Bill Athey, people who will always be part of my life and if they lived near me then I would go for a beer with them and mix with them socially.

I have always been wary about opening up to people, but there are three guys I can talk to about anything. One is Trevor Smith, who was my best man and also one of my teammates at Derbyshire. He still lives in Derby and was somebody I connected with when we were county teammates, and I have kept in touch with him ever since and see him whenever I can.

Then there is Pete Evans, who used to be an auctioneer but now works for himself. He lives in Leicester and is somebody I play a lot of golf with and he, too, has become a very good friend.

And finally, there is Charlie Dagnall. I am godfather to his daughter, Beatrix.

My problem is that I have always found it difficult to trust people and let them in because of what has happened to me, both as a child and as a cricketer. While I was playing, there were people who befriended me because of who I was. They obviously believed it did their reputation some good for them to be able to say they were friendly with an England cricketer – personally, I could never work that one out, but there you go. Over time it became more and more difficult to work out whether somebody wanted to get to know Phil DeFreitas the human being or Phil DeFreitas the cricketer, and it is clearly important to me to be able to distinguish the difference.

Would they be my friend if I wasn't a professional cricketer? When I meet people I try to work them out, going with my gut instinct and I am right about them more than 90% of the time. I know within seconds whether or not I am going to be able to get on with somebody.

Because of all the back-stabbing I was subjected to during my county career, I tend to keep people at arm's length because many of the people who let me down were individuals I considered to be friends and I don't want to be hurt like that again.

Sometimes you get into company with people who will start talking about friends they have known since school, and that is something I struggle to get my head around. I have lived a pretty nomadic sort of a life so there was never really going to be a chance of me being able to keep that sort of a friendship going. In any case, I left the boys I went to school with behind me – I wanted to leave it behind because it was a bad time in my life. Fortunately, my life took me in a different direction.

The top and bottom of it for me is that having friends and trusting people is difficult and I am certain that I will have turned away from people that I could easily have got close to. It is a regret that I have found it difficult to let people in, but on the other hand, the people who feature in my life make me very happy and I wouldn't swap them for anything.

We all have regrets, moments that we wish we could relive, things we wish we hadn't done or said.

I was in Sydney with England in the 1994-95 Ashes series and hadn't played in the Test there because I was injured, although I did feature in the others. I did 12th man duties and we lost, despite making a good fight of it. Towards the end of the match, I became aware of lots of Australian kids coming out with some truly foul language, and all of it was being directed towards us. There was one particular group and they were very aggressive, and quite menacing. It was horrible.

At the end of the match we were all in the changing room, disappointed at having lost and angry at the abuse we had been subjected to, and we all wanted to get out of there as quickly as possible. A bat was brought in for us all to sign – this was and still is a common thing to be asked to do.

It was handed to Tuffers and instead of writing his own name, he put: 'Mickey Mouse', and then it came to me, and I wrote 'sod off'. I was just messing about, and was planning to rub it out and replace it with my signature but I was distracted and the next thing I knew was that the bat had disappeared. I consoled myself with the thought that somebody must have removed my scrawl, and I didn't think anything more of it.

We then went off and played the other Tests and eventually flew back home. Several months went by and then, out of the blue, I received a phone call from the ECB. "Hello Phil, do you remember signing a bat during the Sydney Test?"

"Yes," I replied.

"Well somebody wrote 'sod off' on it, and having looked at everybody's hand-writing, we have narrowed it down to three of you – yourself, Tuffers and Graeme Hick."

Obviously, I knew it was down to me, but I couldn't bring myself to own up, so I said: "No, it's nothing to do with me."

The bat, by the way, had ended up with somebody involved with the Australian Cricket Board, who wrote to the ECB to complain. It goes without saying that they couldn't ignore it.

I put the phone down and tried to convince myself that this was just somebody having a laugh and that it would all go away, but about a month later I received a letter from the ECB informing me that they were going to send the bat to a hand-writing expert to determine who was responsible. Talk about an over-the-top reaction!

I read the letter in disbelief and thought: "This is just ridiculous, and all because of something I have done in the heat of the moment and was obviously stupid." All that they had to do was get a rubber or a piece of sandpaper and remove it, but no – a hand-writing expert! Apart from anything else, I was staggered that they were willing to spend so much money to get their answer.

A few more weeks passed and then they came back to me and told me that they believed I was the culprit, so I was called into Lord's to face the powers-that-be of the ECB.

"Can you explain why you did it?" I was asked.

"Look, it was me, but I was very angry, I was upset, I didn't play in the Test, I was getting lots of abuse from school kids who were saying things that were much worse than anything that is written on this bat. I just snapped. It was a mistake, I know it was, but I had planned to scribble off what I had written but the bat disappeared before I could. I didn't mean to offend anybody and I apologise for my actions. The reason I didn't own up when I was asked if it was me was because I was embarrassed."

They fined me £2,000 - £1,000 for the 'offence' and the rest to pay for the handwriting expert. I walked away shaking my head, but do you know what? I accepted the punishment because I knew that I shouldn't have done it, and it remains one of the biggest regrets of my life and my career. Writing 'sod off" on the bat was bad enough, but failing to accept responsibility for my actions was much worse.

It may or may not be coincidence that after playing one Test against West Indies in 1995, I was never again selected to play another for England.

I have stressed more than once in the preceding pages that I loved to play cricket, no matter where, no matter who for. That being the case, the other big regret would be the times when I made up my mind that I didn't want to play. Normally, I would have walked from one end of the land to the other to represent England or my county but there would be the odd time when it might be a nothing game and I really didn't want to bowl, so I would give my captain an excuse for sitting it out.

It was only as I was approaching the end of my career that I found myself sitting down and thinking: "You know what Daffy, you really should have bowled in those matches because there were dozens of young cricketers who would have given their right arm for the chance to do what you have done." Fortunately, I can put my hand on my heart and say I only did that on a few very, very rare occasions, but I wish now that I had simply made the effort. You are a long time retired (hopefully), but you never get those days back, and those are the things you have to live with, knowing that if you had bowled a few overs then you might well have turned the game around.

By and large though, my conscience is clear and I know that when I was out there, I consistently gave my all and left nothing in the locker. You have to make the best of your career, and I believe that I did.

But perhaps my biggest playing mistake, and thus the biggest regret of my career, was leaving Lancashire. I did it for the right reasons, trying to save my marriage, but I was happier at Lancs than I was at any other stage of my career, and when I look at what happened when I moved to Derbyshire and then on to Leicestershire, is it any wonder that I wish I had the chance to review that decision?

My teammates at Old Trafford were a great bunch of lads, I enjoyed living in the North-West and, of course, I had success with Lancashire.

The game of cricket has mainly been pretty good to me and I would hope that it will remember me as somebody who always gave everything he had and who made the most of his talents. I had a good career, and hopefully others will agree with that. With few exceptions, I was always passionate about my cricket – I pray that the people who watched me perform with bat and ball gained a sense of that, and realised what it all meant to me. I have never prejudged anybody based on their background, where they were from or the colour of their skin.

Cricket changing rooms are generally great places because they always contain such a fabulous cross-section of characters and personalities – hopefully I made a positive contribution to that atmosphere with England, Lancashire, Leicestershire and Derbyshire. Changing rooms contain people from many different cultures, and they always seem to find a way to get on with one another; sometimes people speak their minds, but that is fine. It often occurred to me that politicians would do well to spend some time in a cricket changing room, just to see how it is possible for such an eclectic mix of people to exist alongside one another. Society could learn much.

The banter is something I still miss. I am sometimes asked if I regret not having been born 20 years later because the guys who represent England today are so well rewarded but the way I answer that is quite simple: when I was making way on the international arena, there were players who were 20 years older than me saying that they wished they could be playing in my era.

It is the way things go – wages increase, as do sponsorship opportunities and various other rewards available to modern sportsmen. Did anybody believe that a professional footballer playing in England would ever earn £200,000 a week? I doubt it, although all logic dictates that those sums of money cannot possibly be sustainable, and if you earn so much, do you ever truly appreciate anything that comes your way?

Besides, if I had played at a different time then I would have missed the opportunity of competing with and against some of the greatest players the world has ever seen. The best I played against, and with, was Wasim Akram, the Pakistani fast bowler who was at Lancashire at the same time as me. He was a match winner, with bat and bowl, and he was a terrific person and a good friend, somebody who was always there for me.

Right up there, too, were Viv Richards and Malcolm Marshall. They were just special players and, again, delightful people. And what about some of my old England teammates? There is nothing new or original to be said about Ian Botham, but I also played alongside the likes of David Gower, who was one of the most elegant batsmen I ever saw, Graeme Thorpe, Graham Dilley, Chris Broad, Graham Gooch, Allan Lamb and Alex Stewart. It reads like a *Who's Who?* of England cricket, and I was lucky enough to share the stage with them.

It is unfair to pick out one or two, but each of them stick in your mind for different reasons – Broad was not the most elegant of batsmen but he would rather die than give his wicket away; Goochie put in endless hours of practice to achieve what he did, and Gower's touch was sublime, even when it came to practice sessions. And that brings me back to the point I was making about coaching – every player is different and goes after their targets in different ways. A good coach will know that.

CHAPTER 37
HAPPY EVER AFTER

I am in a good place now. I am happily married, I have a job I enjoy and I have two wonderful sons and a daughter but, professionally, I have itchy feet. You have got this far with my story so by now you know that I have always needed somebody to put a reassuring arm round my shoulder and tell me I am appreciated, that I am doing a good job. I have always been that way, still am and always will be.

At present I am the cricket professional at Magdalen College School in Oxford. I coach boys between the ages of 11 and 18, and I also go to the feeder schools to spread the message that Magdalen is not just a great academic school, but that it has a wonderful sporting pedigree too.

During the winter months I help out the staff with other sports, including football, rugby and hockey. Everybody at the school has gone out of their way to make me feel welcome. There is a great atmosphere around the place and I am delighted to be a part of it.

One of the other things I do, and thoroughly enjoy, is to work as an ambassador for the Professional Cricketers' Association, attending golf days, Kwik cricket, dinners, corporate days and that kind of thing. I still play the game and have captained Lashings World XI, playing club sides all over the country.

Throughout my long career I achieved a great deal and played at the very highest level for 20 years, which is not something that many cricketers can say, particularly those who bowl at any sort of pace. To keep going for that length of time I had to work hard and of course it became more difficult as I grew older, but I stuck with it because I loved what I was doing. Luck played a huge part too – many players are dogged by injury but, on the whole, I remained pretty fit throughout my playing days.

Because of what I have been through in my life and career, I have a huge amount to offer. Sometimes I sit down and reflect on how odd it seems that I, who hated school, get so much pleasure and enjoyment from working in a private school. I am fortunate to be working with some very bright kids and I tell them to make the most of it, and not to throw away the opportunities that are being presented to them.

The boys I coach learn stuff that they wouldn't normally pick up until they leave school, and that is a matter of pride for me. With me, they get fast-tracked in the right direction – I have made the mistakes myself so I can spot them in others and identify how they can be fixed. I wouldn't ever want to put pressure on any youngster, but I have coached a few boys who could make it all the way to the England team.

Working with schoolboys is incredibly rewarding but I would be a liar if I said that I wasn't interested in coaching a county side or getting involved with the England team. The set-up is really professional now, everything is done the right way and if you have a problem, whether it be with your game or in your private life, there will always be somebody you can turn to for guidance.

You work with what you have, offering advice, coaching and guidance where required, and you bring in one or two new players. It is easy for a coach to spend a fortune bringing in a recognised batsman or bowler;

it is far more difficult to bring out the talent in young players already on the books or to see the potential in youngsters who might be playing for rival counties. If it was easy, every county would win every game. The best coaches work with what they have and make them better – that is what I have always resolved to do; it is what gets my juices flowing.

Counties should be more honest with their fans and explain to them why certain decisions are being taken or have been taken. Let's say, for example, that a new coach is appointed and comes into the club, usually armed with a three-year plan. What the fans want is success – it is the same in every sport. Nobody wants to support a club that keeps losing, but maybe they don't mind losing a few games if they can see some progress towards a brighter future and can see that young players are being allowed to develop.

What happens instead is that the coach realises he has to deliver success within that three-year period or else he will be out on his ear and will be looking for a new job. Would it not be better if they were straight with the fans from the start and gave an honest assessment? 'I have looked at the playing staff and I know what has to be done to improve results. Give me some time and then judge me on whether or not you consider that we have made some progress.'

We see too many coaches and players coming in and promising the earth when the people who have spent their lives following the club want nothing more than not to be treated like they were idiots. Don't promise them the title or a cup unless you can guarantee that you will be able to deliver. And if the county is still struggling as badly after the new coach has introduced all his changes, there is an argument for saying that he doesn't deserve to still be in the job anyway.

I look around at the present crop of coaches and it is clear that Andy

Flower possesses some special gifts. He has done very well with England and is obviously his own man. It could be argued that he is fortunate to have a great Test side, but that didn't happen by accident. At different times, Flower has been under pressure to drop this player or that player, but he has shown faith and stuck with bowlers and batsmen who, in a previous generation, would have been dropped and perhaps never seen again at international level. The sign of a good coach is that he remains true to his beliefs and gives his players absolute backing and support.

When Les Stillman first arrived at Derbyshire he had this uncanny knack of knowing exactly what to say and when to say it. "Daffy, this is your session. I can just feel it," he would say.

And then, what do you know, but I would go out and take a few critical wickets and turn the game. Now you can read what you want into that – was that just good man-management and did I go out and perform better because of the confidence he had given me? Or should he have been doing the National Lottery? I opt for the former.

I have picked up things from various people. I would be playing for Leicestershire and would have spent the day toiling in the field, and maybe picked up two or three wickets, and we would come in for the tea break and I would be shattered, but Ken Higgs would come up to me and ask: "Daff, do you love taking five wickets?"

"Yes Ken, of course I love taking five wickets."

"Well, the new ball is due after tea, so go to the captain and tell him you want it and that you are not going to come off until you have got this lot out, then you will get your five wickets."

That is the point at which the mental side takes over from the physical side, and it was uncanny how often I would pick up those wickets. He would do the same thing with batsmen who were dismissed in the 70s or

80s. "You don't like hundreds then?" It meant that the next time they got to the crease and reached 70-odd, his words would be going around their heads and they would be absolutely determined to hang around and score a century. It was genius man-management, saying the right thing to the right man at the right time.

That is the way I am trying to teach the boys in my charge. You need to know what makes them tick, so I find out how they are getting on at school, what their background is and all that kind of stuff. I guess you would call it lifestyle coaching. Generally, if they are doing well at school they will do well on the cricket field. If they are unhappy at school or at home, they will usually struggle with sport.

I am convinced that if a boy is physically fit, then he will do better with his schoolwork. I would never tell a boy that he has to do this or that; all that I can do is provide him with the information and hope that he will listen. One of the most satisfying feelings is when you give a youngster some help or advice and you can see that they have taken it on board and that it has helped their batting or their bowling. As a coach, or a teacher if you prefer, there is nothing to top that.

I take on board new coaching methods, and if I can stop a young cricketer from making the sort of mistakes I did then I feel that I have achieved something truly worthwhile.

So cricket continues to dominate my life, but please don't run away with the idea that I am obsessed by it. I relax by playing golf – some people consider it a misnomer to talk about golf being a form of relaxation because it is such a frustrating sport, but I have never let it wind me up. I don't have an official handicap so I tend to play off nine and am regularly accused of being a bandit – I am told that I should be off six but I don't play often enough to justify that sort of figure.

I am also fascinated by history. Early in my career I used to go round looking at stately homes, and I was entranced – you walk round and try to imagine what life was like there hundreds of years ago. For me, it is not about getting the information, it's just about letting my imagination run riot. If you sit down and talk to me about history, you will bore me, but let me loose in a big old house and I am in my element.

You never know what is around the corner. If a county job comes along or the chance to work with England, all well and good, but do you know what? I would be happy to carry on working with in schools, helping them to improve.

My old mate Phil Tufnell had his life turned around thanks to *I'm A Celebrity, Get Me Out Of Here*, which brought him to a whole new audience, as well as showing a different side of him to the man fans thought they knew. He has made the most of the chance that was offered to him and I am delighted to see him doing so well now.

Would I appear on a show like *I'm A Celebrity*? Well, you never say never, I suppose, and if the opportunity came along then I would probably take it, even though I regard it as the toughest of the reality programmes. I reckon that I would be able to cope with having to eat bugs, but the thought of tackling some of those trials fills me with horror. It would be hard work, but I figure that you have just got to be yourself – that's what Tuffers did. What you see with him is what you get, and I have always been the same.

People used to say that I wore my heart on my sleeve, but I have always believed that you should show people how you are feeling. I do it because I care, whether it be on a cricket field or in life. Sometimes people would misread it and get the impression that I was angry but it was because I was disappointed.

CHAPTER 38
I MUST HAVE GOT
SOMETHING RIGHT

I have never been one to blow my own trumpet, and I hope that message has come across as I have told you my story. It is the way other people see you that means the most because it gives you an idea of the impact you have had on their lives and the impression they have of you.

In 2008, Charles Dagnall, a former teammate at Leicestershire, offered to write me a reference and I reproduce it here only because it explains better than I could ever manage myself some of the things that make me tick. I thank Charles hugely for the following words:

"Over the past ten years of knowing Phillip, I have found him to be the model of professionalism both in and out of the cricketing arena.

"When I first met him, I was impressed no end by how a player of his magnitude in the game could be so approachable, good humoured yet totally focused when it came to his sport. As a senior former England player, one might expect that his final years in county cricket would have been a time to slow down. Far from it. In his dedication to fitness, training and structured practice, he continued to prove that his quality as an all-round cricketer was permanent.

"During this time he took it upon himself to use his vast knowledge of the game to coach the junior members of the side, with whatever facet of their game was lacking, and it was done with huge enthusiasm. The most impressive aspect of this was that whenever a player found himself struggling, Phillip would try every avenue, both physically and mentally, to get the player back on the right path. To find someone who can use their knowledge of cricket at the highest level and explain it simply and thoroughly to junior players is a rare commodity. I played county cricket for eight years before retiring through injury, and I genuinely believe it wouldn't have been half that had it not been for Phillip's help and guidance. There are a lot of cricketers who would say the same thing.

"The other major quality that Phillip displayed was patience. It can be easy for those who have played Test cricket to get frustrated with their pupils' inability to grasp a certain concept. The upshot being that the player gets disheartened, loses confidence, loses the ability to take on board coaching and thus regresses. This has never been the case in the years that I have known Phillip as a player or coach. No matter how long it may take (depending on the player) he finds a way to make the player feel comfortable.

"I was lucky enough to play under him when he was captain at Leicestershire. He was forthright, inventive and was not afraid of making the tough decision. This manner worked instantly with the players as they always knew where they stood, and were never left in the dark. Off the field, he demonstrated the class expected of a county cricket captain."

I have always tried to behave in the correct way, on and off the field, and if I achieved that and if, as Charles says, I have helped some cricketers along the way then I am happy that I have done something right.

www.apexpublishing.co.uk